THE SECRETS OF PROFITABLE CLOUD KITCHEN

18 Secrets and Effective strategies to Build, Launch and Scale your Cloud Kitchen Business and Make it Profitable within 90 days.

SHEETAL SALUNKHE

ACKNOWLEDGMENT AND DEDICATION

I thank the universal energy that has driven me to create this amazing book.

I want to thank my supportive husband Sandeep, my loving daughter Sameera and my precious mother and father. Thank you, family for believing in me and supporting me throughout my food-entrepreneur journey.

Next, I want to thank my mentors Dr. Abhinav Saxena for guiding me on my food-entrepreneurship journey and Mr. Mitesh Khatri who inspired me to write a book.

I want to thank my designer team for assisting me in beautifying this book and make it presentable to my aspiring readers.

Finally, I want to dedicate this book to you and to all my readers who are committed to learn and become successful food entrepreneurs.

CONTENTS

AUTHOR'S NOTE: WHY READ THIS BOOK?

'Can you please guide us how did you start cloud kitchen business? Can I also do this business? I always wanted to do something on my own, get into a business, but don't know how to do it? How long I will do this corporate job? Want a break. How long will I stay at home doing nothing? Tell us what steps you followed. Is this business profitable? How to make profits?'

Am I reading your mind? Who am I? An ordinary woman, working in IT field for almost 17+ years, has no background of food/any business but always had a strong desire to become an entrepreneur, learnt, prepared, built and successfully launched a cloud kitchen and went on to scale it up with three brands and emerged out as a successful food entrepreneur. That is me.

With more and more people living in cities, adopting to digitization, and having busy work schedules, there is a growing need for convenient food options that can be delivered to their homes. The recent pandemic hit has forced people to ordering food online and people are used to it now.

If you are a passionate and enthusiastic person about Food and Business around it, does not matter if you are a male/female, working/not working professional, a housewife, has or does not have any business background, then Cloud kitchen is the easiest, and low risk entry point to become a food entrepreneur.

Many restaurants and other food business models have started to adopt the cloud kitchen model to reach a larger customer base and increase their revenues.

I want to personally promise you that this book reveals secrets behind the effective strategies to Build, Setup and Scale your own cloud kitchen business and make it profitable within 90 days. These secrets and strategies are from my own business experiences.

This book acts as a handbook for any established food entrepreneur or a person having no business background but has a strong desire to become a successful Food Entrepreneur.

So, are you ready to make that important decision to live your dream? Are you ready to live your passion? Are you ready to learn and transform yourself and see yourself as a successful food entrepreneur? I heard you saying YES! Ok then, let us go to the next chapter to know my true story and grab all the secretes from then following chapters....

MY STORY: HOW CLOUD KITCHEN BECAME MY ENTRY POINT IN FOOD BUSINESS

In early 2020, the entire world was hit by COVID-19 and every country, every state, every city and every other person just like you and me was shaken up and was forcefully locked down in homes. All the offices opted for Work-From-Home and majority of employees started working from their respective home. I was working in IT field and was also excited to get an option to work from home. With entire family at home, initial few days were just to sync in and get comfortable with changes in work culture. Everything outside, hotels/restaurants were closed, and we had to cook at home varieties of dishes for our beloved family. Being a good cook and passionate about serving good food to my family, I started surfing the YouTube channels on recipes to upgrade my culinary skills. As my family and personally me also, has more liking towards the non-veg food, I started preparing different Maharashtrian Chicken recipes. My family was loving the variety and taste. I used to click photos of the dishes and put it on WhatsApp status. On seeing these tempting food photos, my friends used to say, *'aree yaar, agar tu Swiggy/Zomato pe hoti to tumse hi khana order karate! Looks so tempting!'('If you would have been available on Swiggy/Zomato, we would have ordered food from you for sure.')* I used to get very happy and motivated with this appreciation.

One of my neighbourhood family had tough time w.r.t the food during the lockdown period as the lady of the house, my very good friend, was stuck in USA almost for four months and the rest of her family – her husband and son were here in our residential complex. Her family was not getting good, hygienic food from outside as everything was shutdown. My friend used to see the food photos on my WhatsApp status and one fine day, she asked me, *'anyhow you are cooking non-veg for your family, so can you cook a little extra for my family as well and provide them food and they will pay for it?'* Wow, I was thrilled and overwhelmed with the idea of someone approaching me with an opportunity to monetize my cooking skills! Although I was bit doubtful initially, but I decided to go ahead and provide them food at least from humanity point of view. That is where my journey of selling food online started! My friend's family was my first and regular customer. I started making money by getting orders on WhatsApp and phone call, cooking at my home kitchen and delivering food to their doorsteps. That is what is called cloud kitchen!

My journey of Food Entrepreneurship started from my very own home kitchen. This journey became a marathon and continues to be.... Isn't it exciting? Isn't it familiar to you when you get appreciated for the delicious food you cook for your family? How many times the thoughts ran from your mind to sell the food and earn money? I am pretty sure, every now and then you had this thought popping up. But you supressed it saying, *I do not know how to start it? How can I get into a business? Is it profitable?*

But I was thrilled with the regular orders flowing in for quality food. How do I convert it into bigger scale? This thought was just a seed, beginning of my Food Entrepreneurship. In the next following chapters, I will tell you how I nurtured this seed and converted it into a commercial cloud kitchen setup and successfully running 3 brands from a single cloud kitchen setup.

KNOW BEFORE YOU START YOUR JOURNEY

Before getting started on this journey, let us first understand what is the future of food business? What is cloud kitchen? And who can do it?

B.1. What is the Future of food business?

Food is one of the topmost essential need of humans. In 2023, the World population increase is estimated at 67 million people per year. That is huge. India is top most country currently with highest population in the world. The Indian government's focus on "Atmanirbhar Bharat" (self-reliant India) and "Vocal for Local" campaigns, which aims to promote and support local food production, distribution, and consumption, is expected to have a positive impact on food business in India. The organic and natural food market is expected to see strong growth as consumers in India become more health-conscious and interested in sustainable food options.

The Indian food industry is heading towards change along with digitalization to its core. Creative service offerings are launched, health and safety are being prioritized, standardised and operations are becoming less expensive as the industry is moving towards chef less and less labour-intensive models. All these changes will elevate customer experience and set new standards for the industry in the post-Covid era. Online food delivery platforms such as Zomato/ Swiggy, Uber Eats and e-commerce in India are projected to experience significant growth as more and more consumers become comfortable with ordering food online and having it delivered to their homes. These food delivery platforms have made it easier for customers to order food online from a variety of outlets and have it delivered to their doorsteps. The FnB (food and beverage) market in India is expected to continue to grow, driven by factors such as population growth, urbanization, and rising disposable income. In addition, the COVID-19 pandemic has accelerated the growth of food delivery in India as people have been looking to avoid going out and ordering food online and are now used to have the food at the comfort of their homes.

According to a report by research firm RedSeer, the online food delivery market in India is expected to reach $4.9 billion by 2023, growing at a CAGR of over 20%. The report also states that the food delivery market in India is expected to grow even faster in the post-COVID era, as more people will be ordering food online to avoid crowded places. Indian Food Market is forecasted to reach 95.75 Billion $ by 2025 with a CAGR {Compounded Annual Growth Rate } of 10.3% between 2020 – 2025.

Overall, the demand for home delivery of food in India is expected to continue to grow in the coming years, driven by changing consumer behaviours and the growing popularity of online food delivery platforms.

In India, the cloud kitchen model is becoming increasingly popular as more and more people are ordering food online. Many restaurants and other food business models in India are starting to adopt the cloud kitchen model to reach a larger customer base and increase their revenue. Some popular examples of cloud kitchens in India include Rebel Foods, which operates a network of virtual kitchens in different cities.

Going by statistics, with strong gust from food delivery and now the pandemic, the cloud kitchen market is poised to grow rapidly to $3 billion by 2023.

B.2. Why cloud kitchen?

As you can understand, a cloud kitchen can be started from your very own home kitchen, proving it to be low investment, less staff requirements, quickly scalable and profitable business model. With its limited/smaller working space, it provides safer environment for the customers to trust in hygiene.

Even when I shifted my cloud kitchen from home setup to commercial setup, the investment was very low as compared to setting up a full-fledged restaurant, with cool ambience and necessary staff.

Without worrying about footfall, the cloud kitchen setup can be operational from anywhere serving the customers within 4 to 10Km area. Online presence is what matters in case of cloud kitchen setup.

The basic idea of running a cloud kitchen is to reach to maximum customers online rather than many customers visiting your outlet offline. That is why the setup/ operational cost reduces drastically as compared to setting up a conventional restaurant business, saving on rent of the property and the same saving can be used for paying to minimum required staff's salary and majority on marketing of your brands. More the marketing, more the reach to customers, more leads, more orders and thus generate more revenues leading to more profits.

The cloud kitchen model is easily scalable. I am running my three food brands from a single cloud kitchen setup in 200Sq.Ft area. Depending on the available space, the cloud kitchen can be scaled up to run multiple brands from one place. Unlike the restaurant setup, cloud kitchen setup does not need more staff like waiters, multiple chefs so there is heavy cost saving on the salary of staff. We will see the strategies in details to hire the minimum required staff in the coming chapters.

With increased digitization and vast popularity of food delivery aggregators like Swiggy and Zomato, people are used to order food online and get delivery at home to enjoy the food at their home comfort. Before ordering food, people do search for a specific food type on Google, read about the reviews and check on Swiggy and/or Zomato for the ratings and reviews to know about the kind of food served from this place. Hence your brand's online positioning on the social media such as Google, Instagram, Facebook, YouTube, Food Aggregators is very important. With increased use of social media by more and more people, it's easier for the food brands to connect with and reach to more and more customers easily. Using the right strategies of effective free and paid online and offline marketing, the cloud kitchens can attract more customers and generate more revenues. We will explore these marketing strategies and secrets in the coming chapters.

B.3. What is Cloud Kitchen?

Having understood the tremendous growth potential of food business and the cloud kitchen model, let us first understand what is a Cloud Kitchen?

It is also known as virtual kitchen, dark kitchen or ghost kitchen. This food business model allows entrepreneur to minimize the operational costs by eliminating the need for a physical storefront and dining area. Instead, it focuses more on food preparation and delivery.

The demand for home delivery of food has been increasing in recent years, post COVID-19 era too, and is driven by factors such as increased urbanization, a growing middle class, habituated to home comfort and the rise of online food delivery platforms.

Low start-up cost: The cloud kitchen can be started even from home kitchen setup and can be scaled up further with manifolds. Setting up a cloud kitchen typically requires less investment than setting up a traditional restaurant. There is no need to invest in a physical storefront or dining area with attractive ambience, which can significantly reduce setup costs.

Reach a larger customer base: This model also allows businesses to reach a larger customer base through online delivery platforms and social media platforms irrespective of customers knowing their actual physical location.

Flexibility: Cloud kitchen allows for flexibility in menu offerings and kitchen space. This can be beneficial for new entrepreneurs who may not be sure of their target market, as they can test different types of food and menus to see what works best with their target market.

Scalability: Cloud kitchen model can be easily scaled up as the business grows. This means that as the business grows, the entrepreneur can expand their menu offerings, hire more staff, and increase their kitchen space, without having to worry about the costs of setting up a new physical location. Multiple brands can be operated from a single kitchen.

Cost savings: With cloud kitchen, entrepreneurs save on costs such as rent for huge restaurant space, utilities, and maintenance of a physical space, which is a significant advantage for new businesses. The cost savings can be more efficiently used in right marketing strategies to attract more customers to the business.

Overall, cloud kitchen is a good option for a new or aspiring food entrepreneur, as it offers low start-up costs, the ability to reach a larger customer base, flexibility, scalability, and cost savings. However, it is important to conduct market research and create a solid business plan before starting a cloud kitchen. I will take you through the important secrets of creating business plan in the following chapters.

Read more at: *https://yourstory.com/2020/09/ola-foods-cloud-kitchens-contactless-delivery* from actual cloud kitchen brand like Ola Foods on their views about cloud kitchen and it's growth to get inspired.

It is important to note that operating a cloud kitchen also comes with its own set of challenges which are equally there with other food business models like restaurants, QSR, TakeAways, Food Truck. These challenges are competition, marketing costs and delivery costs. We will discuss on the secrets on how we can overcome these challenges in the coming chapters.

Read an inspiring article from the founders of Rebel Foods on how they focused on setting up kitchens with a focus only on delivery and how technology helped them to expand and scale fast across India. Read more at: *https://yourstory.com/2021/10/turning-point-cloud-kitchen-model-faasos-foodtech-unicorn-rebel-foods*

The first important take away from this article is people associate brands with cuisines so rather than offering multi-cuisine under one brand, have multiple brands for specialised cuisine. The second important take away is: if you want customers to order frequently from you, you need multiple cuisines.

Having read so far, note down 5 top reasons why you want to get into cloud kitchen food business?

Super inspired to become a food entrepreneur? Let me now answer to the question that is popping in your mind right now - Is food business for me? Can I start with this business?

B.4. Who can start Cloud Kitchen business?

If you are the ONE who has a passion for food, a strong work ethic, and a strong entrepreneurial spirit then irrespective of your gender, profession or educational background, definitely you are well suited to start a food business. Majority of people will have the following questions in mind before starting the food business.

1. Which is the right age to get into food business?

2. I am a housewife. Can I get into food business?

3. I am into a corporate job. Can I get into food business?

4. Which educational background should I have for getting into food business?

And so on…

There is no specific age that is considered the 'right' age to get into the food business. Age is not a limiting factor in starting a food business, as long as you are of legal age to start a business in your country (18 years age in India) and have the necessary skills, experience, and resources to start and run a food business. That being said, starting a food business can be challenging and demanding, so it's important to be realistic about your own abilities, experience, and resources. It is always beneficial to get an experience in the food industry and have a clear vision and plan for the business, and necessary funding and knowledge about the resources required.

There is no specific educational degree/ background you need to hold to get into food business. A strong entrepreneurial spirit and passion for food are the basic essential qualification needed to get started off with your food entrepreneurial journey.

Majority of the women out there aspire to be a Food Entrepreneur and want to convert their hobby/passion for cooking/baking into a career. The major reasons/ benefits that a woman/housewife pursuing their passion for cooking and doing own business includes flexibility to work around other commitments such as family or household responsibilities while pursuing their passion, they gain financial independence, entrepreneurial experience and potential for growth.

A corporate job and a food business are quite different in terms of work environment, responsibilities, and career opportunities. Ultimately, whether a corporate job or a food business is a better fit for you depends on your personal goals, skills, interests and your risk appetite. It is possible to do a corporate job and start a food business at the same time, but it can be challenging to balance the demands of both. This is from my personal experience. I started my food entrepreneurial journey while I was into corporate job. It is important to weigh the pros and cons and plan accordingly, if you decide to pursue both, it's a good idea to have a business plan and set realistic goals for yourself. A good idea is to start small and grow gradually, rather than trying to do too much at once. Are you with me on this? I heard you saying, YES!!

The only qualities that you need to embark while starting off with your food entrepreneurial journey are passion for food, strong work ethics, entrepreneurial mindset, Business Acumen and Creativity.

And in this food entrepreneurial journey you will gain the benefits of financial rewards, sense of accomplishment, personal growth, joy of serving and community building.

So, note down top 5 skills that you possess to start off your food entrepreneurial journey NOW. In the next chapter, come with me to extract the first secret of becoming a successful entrepreneur.

CHAPTER 1

SECRET 1: WHAT IS THE RIGHT MINDSET FOR STARTING FOOD BUSINESS? HOW TO SET THE INTENSIONS RIGHT?

'Anyways you are cooking for your family, can you please cook little extra and serve food for my family also and we will pay for it?' Another customer on a phone call said 'you are so kind and soft spoken, I will definitely visit your outlet to have the food.' Another customer said 'I am a patient and old lady, your food is good, home-made type. Can you please have it delivered to my place for my lunch today? I do not know how to order from Zomato.'

Do you sense, the need of providing service here than thinking about how much money will I make? These are the actual scenarios we faced in our business where providing service was the top most priority. What a joy of serving was felt, cannot be described in words. But surely, you can feel it!

This secret is winner of all secrets. Build your foundation strong with this secret. The secret here is, the right intention is always based on serving more and more. Millionaires' mindset is to serve the entire economy. Making millions of money is easy, you must focus on serving and adding value to million people via your products and services. Money will come. Money is always a bi-product of the best quality delivered.

Now that you have decided to Build and setup your own cloud kitchen, it is very important to set the intentions and mindset right. Honestly ask yourself why do you want to start own food business? What is the purpose of starting food business? Is it to earn more and more money? Commercial success? or you want to serve quality and tasty food to millions of people? Your intentions will decide the success of your food brands.

To start your entrepreneur journey right, it is very important to have strong mindset to achieve your goals. As I took on the challenge of being a food entrepreneur, to build the strong mindset, as was told by my mentor, this audio (available on Youtube for free) helped me tremendously. 'The Strangest Secret.' This is a 30min audio clip you will get on YouTube (*https://www.youtube.com/watch?v=QIC7INOqRiI*) In the era of 1955, this audio created the most Millionaires in the world. It has magical effect on your subconscious mind and helps tremendously to build a strong mindset to become a successful entrepreneur. I listened to it twice a day regularly during my initial days of building and launching of my Cloud Kitchen. It does a magic. Do not skip this at any cost!

Note down 'committed' if you are really committed to listen to this audio and are all set to know the secret no 2 in next chapter. Let us dive in.

CHAPTER 2

SECRET 2: WHAT ARE THE LEGAL/ LICENSE REQUIREMENTS TO OWN A CLOUD KITCHEN?

'Is selling food from home allowed/legal? What legal documents should I have to operate my food business?'

I heard you asking questions on similar lines as was asked by many of the acquaintances including customers. Let us unfold the secrets here.

Let us first understand the company and brands concept of the cloud Kitchen. The Company Name is the base/parent of your food business. Under this company name, you can have multiple brands/child/sister company of food depending on the niche.

Like in our case, our company name is SABROSOO FOODS. Under this company name, we have launched three brands named Book My Chicken, Make My Fish and The Wok Delight! Any future brands I will be launching will be under the company SABROSOO FOODS. Most licenses/

legal documents are to be taken on parent company name. Brand Name is the one which is projected in the market. Food aggregators and customers know you and your food by the brand names. Although the license/legal documents are to be taken on company name (such as FSSAI license, PAN card, Bank's Current account) the trademark is to be obtained on the Brand Name/s. Do search for Trademark on Google to know more about it. Trademarking prevents any other entity to use the same brand name as of yours in the market, allowing only your brand name to be present. Do consult your legal advisor / agents available in the market to proceed with brand name trademark activity. It involves additional cost.

The legal or license requirements to own and start a cloud kitchen varies from the Country and state of operation. It is always best to consult your legal advisor to know the mandatory licenses and permits required to establish and operate a food business in your local area.

To start a cloud kitchen in India, following licenses and permits are required, which includes:

1. **FSSAI License:** The Food Safety and Standards Authority of India (FSSAI) license is mandatory for all food businesses, including cloud kitchens irrespective of whether you are starting it from your home kitchen or from a commercial place. Depending on the nature and scale of the operation, the FSSAI registration may be required, or the FSSAI state or central license may

be necessary. This license is obtained very easily by applying online on yourself or via a legal advisor/agent. The government site in India, for the same is *https://foscos.fssai.gov.in/* Normally withing 30 working days, a FSSAI license can be obtained provided all the necessary information and required documents are provided.

FSSAI license is to be obtained on company name. This license is specific for a given location/address/premise from where the food business/cloud kitchen is operating. If you have multiple locations/branches of your cloud kitchen, then you need to obtain multiple FSSAI licenses each per location/branch under the company name.

Under one FSSAI license per location, multiple brands can operate. FSSAI license is location specific. That is a big secret you must be aware of!

FSSAI license is mandatorily required when you tie-up your brands with online food delivery partners/aggregators like Swiggy, Zomato, UberEats. In some countries/states the requirements of these food aggregators may vary. So, consult with the respective food aggregators point of contacts to confirm on their specific needs.

2. **UDYAM certificate:** Also known as Udyog AADHAAR. This certificate is mandatory to carry out any business including cloud kitchen and is provided

by the central Ministry of Micro, Small and Medium Enterprises (MSME).

3. **NoC certificate from Society/Premises:** If starting the cloud kitchen from home or any residential building premises, it is always advisable to get the No Objection Certificate from the society to avoid any objections by the residents to carry out food business from the property. Although it is not a mandatory certificate, but is good to have certificate to avoid any inconveniences later.

4. **GST Registration:** Goods and Services Tax (GST) registration is mandatory for all businesses operating in India, including cloud kitchens. GST registration is required for all businesses with an annual turnover of over Rs. 20 lakhs. It is always advisable to consult your local legal adviser to know more about GST and its applicability.

5. **Trade License:** The trade license is a legal document issued by the local municipal corporation that allows businesses to operate in a particular area. It is mandatory for all cloud kitchens to obtain a trade license from the local municipal corporation.

6. **Fire NOC License:** A fire NOC license must be obtained from the local fire department before starting a cloud kitchen. The license is mandatory to ensure that the kitchen is equipped with necessary fire safety equipment and complies with fire safety guidelines.

7. **Shop and Establishment Act Registration:** The Shop and Establishment Act is a state/City-specific law that regulates the conditions of work and the employment of workers in commercial establishments, including cloud kitchens. Please check with your local legal adviser to understand if it is mandatorily required in your city of operation. Normally, it is mandatory to register under the Shop and Establishment Act within 30 days of starting the business.

8. **Insurance:** Cloud kitchens should have insurance to cover any liability and damages that may arise.

It is essential to obtain all necessary licenses and permits before starting a cloud kitchen to avoid legal complications and ensure compliance with government regulations. Once you apply for the necessary licenses, till the time you obtain them, proceed with other preparation for building your cloud kitchen brand.

Note down the Company Name for your food business and the licenses you are applying for. In the next chapter we will extract the secrets of investment plan for your cloud kitchen.

CHAPTER 3

SECRET 3: WHAT IS THE INVESTMENT REQUIRED TO START A CLOUD KITCHEN?

*'How much money I need to start a cloud kitchen?'
'What should be the budget I should plan to start with
food business?' 'How much investment is required to
start a cloud kitchen?'*

Yes! Yes! All your questions around investment are answered here with the top secrets revealed.

In India/ any country, the investment required to start a cloud kitchen varies majorly depending on several factors, including the location, size of the operation, the equipment needed, staff requirements and other startup costs.

Starting Cloud Kitchen from Home:

The easiest and simplest form of cloud kitchen is to start it from your own home kitchen. That is how we started and experienced its operations before moving into a commercial setup. If you are starting cloud kitchen from your home, the startup cost/investment is as low as possible, as you will be mostly using your home kitchen equipment, saving majorly on the rent. Starting from home means mostly you will be doing the cooking on your own with help of house maids. This also saves a lot of cost on staffing need. Most of the cost, while starting the cloud kitchen from home, is incurred for obtaining the necessary licenses, branding and marketing. If starting from home, the cloud kitchen startup cost can be as minimum as INR 10,000/- to INR 50,000/- (Starting from home, our cloud kitchen startup cost was around INR 35,000/- inclusive of cloud kitchen mentors course fees, Brand Trademarking, Licenses, Branding and marketing costs.)

If you are a new entrant in Food business, always remember the secret, start small, then make it big.

Starting Cloud Kitchen from a Commercial place:

The investment plan/budget need to have following factors covered while starting the cloud kitchen from a commercial place:

1. **Rent/Lease of Operating space:** Renting or leasing a space that can accommodate your kitchen setup and equipment's required pertaining to the food niche is a significant cost. Also consider the deposit amount that you will have to submit to occupy the premises. It

can vary depending on the location and the size of the kitchen. While the deposit amount is one time cost, the rent of the premise is monthly fixed cost.

For a cloud kitchen with single brand, around 200 to 250 sq. ft carpet area is good enough to start off with. In cloud kitchen setup, the dine-in space is not mandatory. This can save majorly on the operating space thus saving on rent/lease of the premises.

Commercially, I started my cloud kitchen in 250 Sq. Ft area with INR 22,000/- rent. Depending on the location/city from where you are starting the cloud kitchen, the rent will vary. For Metro/Tire1 cities like Mumbai, Bangalore, Kolkata, Delhi, consider the range of INR 21,000/- to 26,000/- as the highest range to start with. Accordingly decide the range of rent as you go to Tire2, Tire3, Tire4 cities in India.

2. **Equipment:** You will need kitchen equipment depending on your food niche such as cooking utensils, refrigerators, fryers, grinders, ovens, and electronic/ hardware machines such as CCTV, printer, Internet connection. These are one time investment costs. Try to keep them minimum and essential ones. As you expand your food niche and go multiple locations, these costs need be incurred per location.

3. **Raw Material, Commercial gas, and Packaging cost:** You will also need to purchase related raw materials and supplies such as vegetables, grocery, raw

chicken/fish/meat to prepare your food. A commercial gas connection (two, one is for backup) is required for cooking depending on your food niche. And the related packaging material depending on the food items. These are recurring costs.

4. **Licensing and Permits:** For company setup, you will need to obtain the necessary licenses and permit from local authorities such as the Food Safety and Standards Authority of India (FSSAI), which will incur costs. This cost needs to be incurred per location as you expand your cloud kitchen at multiple locations. These are one time investment cost.

5. **Marketing and Branding:** You will need to promote your cloud kitchen to attract customers. This will include expenses such as creating logo, designing a website (may not be a must at initial startup stage but later), photoshoot of your food dishes, social media posts, reels, and advertising on social media. Online and offline marketing cost also need to be considered. These are recurring/ ongoing costs.

6. **Aggregator Registration:** You will need to register your cloud kitchen brand/s on multiple popular food delivery aggregators like Swiggy, Zomato where the customers can see your brands and reach out/place orders online. These registrations will incur the cost which varies from aggregator platform to platform. These are one time investment cost.

7. **Staff Salary:** when starting commercially, you will need to hire staff. Minimum you need to consider a chef/cook, a kitchen helper cum delivery boy and a utility staff, to help you run your cloud kitchen. As cloud kitchen is majorly run on delivery, a separate delivery boy can be planned once you reach a certain number of orders per day. To make the social media posts/media you need to hire a graphics designer. The staff's salary is recurring monthly cost.

8. **Electrical and Water Charges:** The commercial electricity bill and water utilization bill of local municipality is recurring monthly cost to be considered.

9. **Repair, maintenance and miscellaneous:** While the cloud kitchen setup is in day-to-day operations, you need to consider the repair, maintenance work and the miscellaneous expenses. These are recurring monthly costs.

10. **Insurance, Fire extinguisher:** It is always advisable to have insurance of your commercial setup and fire extinguisher installed at the premises to avoid any unforeseen situations. This is one-time annual cost.

Generally, starting a cloud kitchen in India, commercially, may require an investment ranging from INR 2 lakhs to INR 10 lakhs depending on your city, food niche and the scale of operation. Overall, it's important to conduct a thorough analysis of the costs involved, considering the above points of one-time expenses and recurring/monthly expenses while starting a cloud kitchen in India and plan your budget accordingly. We started our cloud kitchen setup with two brands Book My Chicken and Make My Fish commercially with initial setup cost of around INR 1,92,000/-

In your notepad, make three sections, one for annual one time investment, second for monthly fixed cost and third for monthly recurring/ongoing cost. This will unfold all the secrets behind how much investment/budget is needed for you to start your cloud kitchen in your locality.

So, all set to establish your food brand in the market? Let us begin to unfold the secrets behind building and launching a scalable brand of your cloud kitchen in the next chapter.

CHAPTER 4

SECRET 4: STRATEGIES TO DECIDE THE NICHE- WHAT TYPE OF FOOD TO SELL?

'I cook best parathas, I cook very tasty biryani, I am best at preparing everything. But I do not know what should I start selling? Which food will be in demand? Should I start selling everything?'

I know, you are asking the same questions as was asked by many aspiring food entrepreneurs. Hold on! Hold on! Even though you are good at cooking everything under this sky, or foodie of all types of food items available under the sky, you need to know the secret behind deciding the niche for your food brand. So, let us unfold the secret.

Deciding which type of food to sell can be a challenging task, but it is an essential aspect of running a successful food business. Here are some steps you must take to help you make an informed decision:

1. **List down your food interest:** Remember you decided to get into food business because of your

passion for food and serving the best quality food to the customers. List down all your favourite cuisines / categories of food items that interests you the most. What interests you will take you for longer run in the business. Among all the food types what I and my family love the most is the nonvegetarian food especially Chicken dishes and Seafood. Hence, we zeroed down on non-vegetarian food and dedicated my first two brands to Chicken specials and Seafood Special niche.

2. **Conduct Market Survey:** Conduct market research to identify what interests you, interests' market as well. Identify the gaps in the market and check out what types of food are in demand. If what interests you, does not already exist in the market, then you are launching brand new niche segment into the market. Conduct market survey to check the demand of the niche and how customers will receive the launch of the new niche.

Simple way to conduct this survey is by creating a Google Form (simply google for how to create the Google Form on google.com and you will get the step-by-step guide to do so. It is very simple.) with brief introduction of the Niche you plan to launch into the market. Ask few basic questions/inputs from the people (who are your prospective customers) as which of the food niche (identified as your high interest) they would like to order more often? How often (twice a week?/ Everyday?/ once in Week?/ Twice in fifteen days?

Or occasionally? Use the same form to check which other niche (apart from your high interest niche) they are interested in? (This will help to understand which niche is in demand in your area.) Once you create this Google Form, circulate the Google Form link on the social media platforms like FaceBook, Instagram and your community/friends/relatives WhatsApp groups and ask people to fill up this survey form. Now, the obvious question is why would people fill up this form circulated on social media? So for people to fill up this form, brief them stating you are starting a new food business and to know the demand of food in your area they can help you by filling up this form. On doing so, offer them a lucrative pre-launch offer, such as 50% off on launch of your brand or Buy1 and Get1 free or any other best offer decided by you considering your product line.

Another way of doing the market survey is by using the food delivery services platform's data. Such as on Swiggy and Zomato, look for the outlets in your area serving the food type (niche) that interests you, they had already tagged few food items from their menu as Best Seller. That shows which food is in demand in that area. Most of the people in your area have been ordering that food. Filter out the Best Seller food items. This helps you to finalize your menu items in the specific niche of your interest.

Analyse the market survey report to finalize on, which niche is in high demand in your area. It can be an existing popular niche such as Seafood specials, Chicken Specials, Biryani, Chinese Cuisine, or it can be a missing niche in the current market such as Healthy Food (salad), Momos, Millet Food etc.

3. Which niche you can deliver the best taste?

Now that you have filtered out your high interest niches considering the market demand, check from the filtered-out niche, which niche you can deliver to the best of your ability by analysing the skills and the expertise you and your team has. You should have a good understanding of the food you are selling and be able to prepare it or get it prepared from your staff with a high quality and a perfect taste. Consider the cost and availability of ingredients as it will impact your pricing and profit margins as well.

Secret mantra here- If you are a new entrant in Food Business, zero down on one niche specific one brand. Once you experiment with it and achieve a certain revenue (ideally Rs 3Lacs plus in 6 to 12 months period) you would have gathered enough experience to launch your next brand pertaining to another niche very easily.

By following these simple filtering steps, you can make an informed decision on what type of food (niche) to sell and which type of food is in high demand. This will surely increase your chances of running a successful food business for a long run.

We started our first brand in our high interest niche of Chicken specials which as per the market survey, is in high demand as well, with the brand name Book My Chicken! Post 6 months of its launch and successful run, launched another brand for our high interest niche and in demand food type, Seafood, with brand name, Make My Fish.

So, having grabbed all the secrets from this chapter, list down all the niches of your high interest and in market demand in your area. Finalize one niche (food type) to start off with your first food brand! Congratulations, you completed a major step here towards building and launching your own food brand! In the next chapter, let me explain you the secrets on how to decide on whom to sell! Who are your customers? Stay focused!

CHAPTER 5

SECRET 5: EFFECTIVE STRATEGIES TO DECIDE YOUR TARGET CUSTOMERS – WHOM TO SELL?

'You are selling only chicken specials and seafood special? Why don't you sell breakfast items also? Not keeping snacks items for evening?' Some outsiders questioned.

Can you understand difference in the customer base for our brand's food items vs the customers for breakfast items vs customers for snacks items? The secret here is to know whom to sell your products to. Let us elaborate more on this secret in this chapter. Stay focused!

Deciding on a target market for your food products is a very important and crucial step in developing an effective marketing strategy. It also helps to define the preferred customer of your brand/ food niche and accordingly decide the menu items and pricing of the same. Pay attention! That is very important statement. Read again. 'Deciding menu items and pricing of the same depends on your preferred target customers.'

I am revealing the crucial secrets, please stay focused. Effective strategies to help you determine your target market/audience:

1. **Conduct market research:** Gather information about the market demand for your food products, including customer demographics, buying habits, and preferences. In earlier section of this book, we covered the Market survey (via Google Form). From the same survey, you can also figure out which food type/product is preferred by which target audience.

2. **Unique Selling Points (USPs):** As you have defined or identified the USPs of your food niche, you can very well define who will be the target audience who would prefer these USPs and go for such food items regularly.

   For e.g. for the food niche of Non-vegetarian (chicken food, seafood) the target audience that comes into mind is families, in the age group of 25yrs to 55 yrs., For the food niche of Momos, Chinese or fast food, the major target audience is youngsters.

   Determine what sets your food products apart from competitors and use this to target a specific group of customers. Specific target audience is very important to focus on branding, costing, and marketing as the strategies for all these three things varies based on which audience/customer has been targeted.

For e.g. while considering the chicken specific brand for youngsters, the kebabs, Rolls or chicken burgers will be high USPs. Basis this audience, your brand name (catchy name to connect with youngsters), brand logo will get finalized. Also the portion size and costing of the same will be defined accordingly which will be affordable for the youngsters. Similarly, the marketing and branding need to be around attracting more and more youngsters and offers also need to be defined accordingly. Whereas if you are targeting a chicken brand for families, then chicken meals, chicken gravy dishes, chicken biryani (one plate or KG wise) are your USPs or sellable products as preferred by these target audiences. The brand name, logo should connect with this customer base. The portion sizes and costing of these products need to be defined based on the target audience preferences and marketing of the same is to be directed accordingly. The offers need to be drafted considering the family audience preference.

By now you would have understood how food niche, target customer audience, branding, marketing, menu items, portion sizes and costing are inter-related. Any change in target customer has direct impact on rest all other parameters.

3. **Customer behaviour:** From the market survey, understand your customer's lifestyle, habits, and values, such as health, and eating patterns, to determine the most appropriate target market for your chosen food.

For example, for the chicken food, if you are targeting family audience, their eating patterns would be eating nonveg twice/thrice a week. Accordingly, you can anticipate the ordering pattern. In the family audience also, differentiate between premium customer and lower/middle class customer, you will see drastic change in costing of the menu items to sale these products based on that target audience.

For the same chicken food, if you are targeting the employees, hostilities or PG/bachelors, the customer behaviour, eating pattern will change drastically. This customer type would want chicken thali or complete meal package to be made available on daily basis at a lesser price. So, the costing need to be based on subscription basis (weekly, monthly subscription).

4. **Identify the social media places where target audience is more active:** Leverage social media platforms to promote your food products and get insights into customer preferences and behaviour. Identify the places on social media (such as Instagram or Facebook or YouTube or WhatsApp) where your target audience is more active and reactive to your brand / food items promotions. This will help you to define the strategies for effective branding, marketing on these platforms to reach more and more customers.

With these secrets unveiled, using these strategies, you need to define the most appropriate target audience/market for your food products and develop an effective branding and marketing plan that will effectively reach and engage your potential customers. **Remember, a change in target market will have change in portion size, costing, branding, and marketing of your food items/ brands.** That is why it is very crucial to decide on your target customer before proceeding with Brand Name, Logo, Menu Design, Packaging and Marketing strategies.

Bulb on? Note down the target age group of your target customer. And let us march towards next chapter to know how to name your first baby, your own cloud kitchen!!

CHAPTER 6

SECRET 6: NAME IT RIGHT: HOW TO DECIDE THE NAME FOR CLOUD KITCHEN BRAND.

'The name of your cloud kitchen brand is so catchy, from the name itself I understood, this must be a specialized brand in chicken dishes', 'I just loved the brand name, so different, unique and catchy, Make My Fish!' 'You have named it so rightly, 'The Wok Delight', makes sense for a Chinese cuisine!'

When customers give these compliments, how does it feel? All efforts to finalize the brand name are paid off with great sense of satisfaction! So, let us extract the secrets on how to name your cloud kitchen brands rightly. Are you with me?

As briefed earlier, your company name should be different than your cloud kitchen brand names. Under once company name you can launch multiple brands pertaining to different niches/cuisines with different brand names.

Our company name is SABROSOO FOODS and brand names in market are Book My Chicken, Make My Fish and The Wok Delight. People will remember brand names prominently than the company name.

Company name can be anything of your choice. It can be named after your family member's name, the God/Goddess name you trust in or any generic/symbolic name of your choice to start with. These names can be suffixed with Foods, Kitchen, or Company. For e.g. our company name 'SABROSOO (means delicious) FOODS', you can name it as 'Mom's/<family member's name> Kitchen', or like 'Annapurna Company'.

Secret here is **THE NAME OF YOUR BRAND DETERMINES HOW PEOPLE PERCIEVE YOUR CLOUD KITCHEN** and that is why it is very important to choose a name that goes with your brand image and that communicates the niche/type of food you are selling. People buy, not only the food, but the brand. People remember Brands.

Deciding the perfect brand name for your niche can be a challenging task but is certainly achievable if you follow the below steps to help you choose/finalise your brand name:

Follow the Brand name theory:

Brand Name should be:

1. **Unique:** Brand name should be unique and should stand out in the market. There should not be sounds like or like other existing brand names in the market.

Or else people will get confused. The marketing efforts you put in for your brand will benefit other existing food brands whose names sounds like your brand name. So be unique and distinguishable in the market.

When we decided to name our brands as Book My Chicken and Make My Fish, it was so unique in the food industry and was clearly distinguishable for the niche. Customers were attracted to the catchy brand name and told me upfront that the names are catchy and took our attention on food aggregator platforms and from the names itself we thought it must be the specialized brand in chicken specials and seafood special segments that's why we ordered from this place. All the efforts put in to finalize the brand names was paid off when customers made these remarks!

2. **Convey niche:** From the name of the brand itself, people should understand what type of food to expect from this brand. The name of your cloud kitchen brand should convey the niche clearly. For e.g. our brand name Make My Fish, clearly indicates it serves seafood. Another brand name 'Book My Chicken' clearly indicates, it sells chicken specials.

    Some other brand name examples where niche is clearly communicated in its names are 'Behrouz Biryani', 'Momo Mia', 'The Wok Delight', 'Chinese Wok', 'Idli express', 'Herbs on Pizza', 'Marky Momos' to name a few.

It's very important to go niche specific while naming your brand name. Customers may not remember/ look for brand names while searching for the food online but they will surely know what type of food they want to have. Like people in your area will search for 'best seafood in Thane', 'outlets providing best momos in Vartak Nagar Thane west', 'best chicken saoji in vartak nagar, thane west', 'best chicken biryani in Viman Nagar, pune'. The more your brand is niche specific, the more likely its searchable by the customers and hence reachable for orders.

When asked customers how did you get our outlet number or got to know about our outlet, majority of them said, we searched for 'best seafood near me' or 'best chicken dishes near me' or 'best Chinese in my area' and your brand name came first on Google and from there we got the outlet number and address. Wow, feeling goosebumps!

3. **Radio friendly:** The brand name should be radio friendly. It should be simple to pronounce, to spell and to type. After hearing to your brand name, it should not be prone to spelling mistakes while customers are typing it on Google or food aggregators to search for it. It should be easy to remember so that chances are high for customers to directly search for or recall your brand name next time they want to order from your outlet.

4. **Web friendly:** Check if the website is available with the brand name. like for our brand's name, we looked

for the website bookmychicken.in on GoDaddy and it was available at a lower cost. Also try to keep the links/names same on all the social media platforms so that it becomes easy for people to remember/search your brand specific data on social media.

For my brand Book My Chicken, the social media details look like as:

Facebook: *https://facebook.com/bookmychicken.in*

Instagram page: *https://instagram.com/bookmychicken.in*

Youtube channel: *youtube.com/bookmychicken*

For my second brand Make My Fish, the social media details look like as:

Facebook: *https://facebook.com/makemyfish.in*

Instagram page: *https://instagram.com/makemyfish.in*

Youtube channel: *youtube.com/makemyfish*

For my third brand The Wok Delight, the social media details look like as:

Facebook: *https://facebook.com/thewokdelight.in*

Instagram page: *https://instagram.com/thewokdelight.in*

Youtube channel: *youtube.com/thewokdelight*

Clearly it demonstrates what is meant by Web friendly. Understanding the secrets?!! Huh!!

5. **Protectable:** Check if the brand name is protectable. The brand name or part of brand name should not have a copyright on it by someone else. If someone has already trademarked it, you cannot use it. Similarly, once you copyright/trademark your brand name, nobody else can use it. There is government website to check if the brand name is available for your usage or whether it has been already trademarked. Refer to *https://ipindiaonline.gov.in/*

   It is always better to consult your legal advisor to proceed with trademarking of your brand name with government. There are agents who do the trademark registration of your brand names against their charges.

6. **Memorable:** Finally, your brand name should be memorable. It should be easy and simple to remember, to pronounce, to type. People should recall your brand name easily increasing chances of them ordering and re-ordering from your outlet provided you serve tasty and quality food every time.

Majorly two types of Brand Names work wonderfully.

1 word Brand Name: Name related to your cuisine/ Type of food/Niche/theme. It should be catchy with double meaning or have local language meaning. Examples of such brand names could be 'Fishland', 'Burgerrr', 'pizzeria', 'RollMama' etc.

2 or 3 word Brand Names: One unique word related to the cuisine/ type of food/ local area name/county/ city and other words relatable to the audience. Recursive words or rhyming words work wonders to catch the attention. Some of the examples of such brand names are 'Book My Chicken', 'Make My Fish', 'Malvan Tadaka', 'Karwar Katta', 'Momos Corner'

So, got to know all the secrets about naming it right? Then note down the Brand name of your niche specific brand. Congratulations! You just completed naming ceremony of your baby!!

Eager to know the next chapter? It's time to give face to your brand name, that is called, Logo! Let us dive-in to extract the secrets!

CHAPTER 7

SECRET 7: EFFECTIVE STRATEGIES FOR LOGO DESIGN.

'Where from you got the logos designed for your food brands?' 'They are so catchy and resonate to the brand names' 'How much did it cost to design the logo?'

Hold on with your excitement! We will spill all the secrets here!

A Logo for your food brand communicates a lot about your food, quality, and values. A logo should be designed in a way that reflects the brand's identity and values. The logo should also be scalable and should work well across different mediums, such as packaging, websites, and social media places. Overall, the logo should be able to communicate the essence of the brand and help differentiate it from competitors in the market.

Let us understand simple yet secret strategies while designing the Logo for your food brand:

1. **Keep it simple:** The logo should be simple, memorable, and easily recognizable. Your prospective customer audience should connect with the logo instantly. The more you try to make it designer with complex designs, it will be difficult for your audience to resonate with it and stay connected with it. Simpler the logo, higher are the chances that your audience will memorize it.

2. **Keep it Readable:** The logo generally has your brand name presented in pictorial manner. The logo should be readable meaning the brand name should be easily recognizable and audience should be able to read it quickly. This way they will memorize it quickly.

3. **Make it Classy:** Simple logo with a classy touch. Your Logo should not be completely local. Give a classy touch to it so that it is scalable.

4. **Have a Clarity in the Logo:** Keep the logo simple and clear. Do not have multiple icons representing your brand name. It complicates the logo. Let the Fonts used are simple and uniform. Do not use multi-fonts. Do not use many colours. Follow the standard colour theory of food industry (Google for it for more details). The most important colours as per the colour theory for food industry are Red, Yellow, and Green. Red colour provokes hunger and is associated with youth. Yellow

colour resonates more to the family audience and green colour represents healthy menu. Green is also associated to echo friendly, vegetarian segment. Using the combination of these colours, design a simple and clear logo with minimum icons with single font. The colours and fonts used in the logo should appeal to the target customers of your brand.

5. **Be Unique, do Not copy:** Do not let your Logo look like any other logo which is already available in the market. If the Logo is look alike of any existing food brand's logo in the market and is protected/ trademarked by that brand, then your brand can come under legal trouble. The audience/customers will easily catch the similarity of logs of two brands. Your brand value will go down in the eyes of the customers.

6. **Logo should be protectable/Trademarked:** Your unique logo should be protectable for the fonts, colours, and designs. Trademarking is essential so that no other brands can copy your logo design, colours, and concept.

Designing the Logo:

Now having understood about the simple secrets of effective logo design, let us see how to get the actual Logo Design done.

1. **Do it Yourself (DIY):** There are online tools available using which you can design your brand logo on your

own. Few tools to name are *http://canva.com, http://looka.com.* Look for the tutorial on Google for these tools or simply follow the steps mentioned on these tools' websites. It is quite easy.

2. **Get it Done:** If you have time constraint or do not want to design the logo by yourself, then you can get it done by hiring the professional designers. *http://fiverr.com* here you will get the freelancer designers who can do logo design for you. Check for their sample work posted on this website, connect with them, understand the cost involved, explain your expectations, and get the logo design done.

   There are social media designers available in the market who does design of logos and social media posts. Check for such social media designers using Goole search, Just Dial (simply call 8888888888) and check out their sample work, check for their charges and work with them to get your unique logo designed.

   Note down the contact details of the logo designers that you will contact for getting your brand's logo design done. Congratulations for a cool brand name and matching brand logo. What next? Now let us finalize the location of your cloud kitchen. What are the secrets behind deciding on the location to attract great sales. Let us figure out in the next chapter.

CHAPTER 8

SECRET 8: EFFECTIVE STRATEGIES FOR SELECTING RIGHT LOCATION FOR YOUR CLOUD KITCHEN

'Is it possible to start cloud kitchen from home?' 'How did you finalize the commercial location to start your cloud kitchen at?' 'How to decide on the location?'

So far, we have decided on what food to sale, Target Market, whom to sell our food to, catchy brand name, Logo, the next immediate task is to finalize the location for the cloud kitchen from where we are going to operate and make sales. How do we do that?

Hold on! Hold On! All your questions have answers in this chapter. The untold secrets are revealed for you to take an informed decision. Let us see the strategic points to finalize your cloud kitchen location for effective sale. You may opt to start your cloud kitchen from Home/residential area or from a commercial property provided following check-points are met.

1. **Target Customer/Audience:** Your Target Market / customer or audience should be within 5km range. This helps to arrange for the delivery of food in cost effective way. If your target audience is beyond 5km range, the delivery cost goes high, time required to deliver food is high and chances of food getting cold are high. Customers would prefer to order from nearby locations. So, need to ensure the target audience/customer is within the range of 5km area.

2. **Should not be in very porch area**: For the cloud kitchen the focus is on delivery model. Customers need not know where exactly the outlet is located. Customers may visit the outlet for pick-up, takeaway or in some cases for dine-in (if you provide a small dine-in space also.) So, the outlet location need not necessarily be situated at a very porch area or on main road. The porch area or main road locations will increase the fixed cost of setup way high. Look for the locations which are accessible (fall within the 5km range of target market) and are not in very porch area. This will drastically save on the rental cost of the cloud kitchen setup.

3. **Minimum area 250 to 300sqft**: If you are a new entrant in food business and starting with one (or two) food brands cloud kitchen, then for the minimum setup requirement the premise should be of 250 to 300 sqft. This will get a kitchen area with comfortable movement, storage area for packaging and raw materials, and parcel dispatching area.

4. **Regular water Supply:** Check if the premise has a regular water supply. It can be continuous water supply or provision to store the water to use throughout the operation timings of the outlet.

5. **Proper Drainage in the property**: Check for the proper drainage system in the property. The wash area of the kitchen needs to be well connected to the drainage system and should not have leakages. If required, get this fixed.

6. **Proper Ventilation**: Outlet property should be well ventilated. Check for the fittings of chimney /exhaust system from the kitchen area of the outlet.

7. **Check for leakage/Damp problems**: Check for overall leakage or Damp problem in the property. Such leakages create problems in hygiene maintenance in the outlet and spoils the raw material storage. If any such leakages in the property, then get it fixed beforehand before starting the outlet operations.

8. **Washing area in the property**: The dish washing area should be within the premises and should have well connectivity with water supply system and drainage system. Preferably have the washrooms inside the premise or in nearby vicinity of the outlet.

9. **Reachable/Parking area for delivery boys:** To give away the deliveries of the food parcel the delivery boys either from the food aggregators (like Zomato/ swiggy delivery boys) or any other third-party delivery

boys (like Dunzo, WeFast, Porter) need to reach the outlet easily. Check the access roads to the premise for easy travel of the delivery boys. Parking space for two wheelers should be available near the outlet.

10. **Proper electricity boards:** Check for the proper electric connectivity to the premise. Have a check-up done by electrician for the required Watts/voltage supply for the electric instruments to be used within the outlet. Ensure separate electric board/meter is available for your outlet. Get the extensions of the electric points/fittings for the ease of operations.

11. **Pest Free:** Before starting the setup of the operation, check if the premise is pest free. The pesticides like ants, cockroaches, lizards spoil the hygiene of the outlet and causes damage to the raw materials. Get the pest control done for the premise before starting the operations. As a good practice, get the pest control done periodically.

12. **If residential, check for permission of society/ apartment:** If you are starting the cloud kitchen from your home or from any residential property, then check for the permission of the society/apartment to have the delivery boys entering the premise, permission for cooking food for commercial sale from home kitchen. Have the necessary permissions or NO objection certificates to proceed further.

These checks will help you to finalize a reasonable and cost-effective location/premise to start off with your cloud kitchen in most hazel free manner. Once the cloud kitchen is in operation, observe the market response, get the feedback from local market, and do the improvements. As the business grows, we can always invest more to go to a different location with bigger space to host multiple brands or to have a bigger dine-in place. But the secret here is always start small and then make it big!

So, look out for the commercial properties to target your target audiences. Reach out JustDial to connect with the real estate agents who can help you get a suitable property.

You are very close to the launch phase of your cloud kitchen brand! Let us meet in next chapter to dig into the secrets of effective branding to socialize your brand! Come with me!

CHAPTER 9

SECRET 9: EFFECTIVE STRATEGIES FOR BRANDING

'When we searched for seafood near me on Google, your brand's name appeared first. Reviews are great. So, we called up to place an order.' 'Digital branding of your brands is superb! Promotional offer posts are attractive, great branding!'

Are you noticing how customers connect with you and your brand at a whole new level? What is the secret behind it? That is what is called effective branding to get noticed and stay in memories of customers.

Branding is a critical aspect of any business, including a food business. Now that we have essentials for your food business ready that is your food brand Name and Logo, let us dive into the secrets that you should know for effective branding of your food business in the market and get noticed by consumers/customers.

Step1: Create Brand USPs: At least have 3 USPs (Unique Selling Points) ready for your food brands. The

USPs will depend on the niche of your brand. Like for example, for our brand 'Book My Chicken' the USPs are 'authentic,' 'hygienic' and 'delicious,' 'homestyle cooked' chicken dishes. Similarly, for your food brand, based on your food niche, define minimum 3 such USPs to highlight to the prospective customers. The USPs can be 'Premium,' 'Homemade,' 'Tasty,' 'Hygienic,' 'Authentic,' 'Unique,' 'Fusion,' 'Affordable' and so one. It should basically describe the quality/characteristic of the food you will be serving under this brand name. This will answer, why customers should buy food from your brand? What is the speciality of your brand? These USPs will serve major role in forming your brand's mission statement to be used in branding.

Step2: Create Mission Statement: Mission statement for your food brand is the statement that explains why you started the food business and what is the long-term vision of your brand. For example, the mission statement for our brand 'Make My Fish' is 'We are on the mission to serve the society with delicious, authentic and hygienic seafood to 1,00,000 families in Vartak Nagar, Thane(W).' It is clearly understandable how beautifully we have used our 3 USPs (as delicious, authentic, and hygienic), food niche (seafood), target customers (families) and target location (Vartak Nagar, Thane West) to form a meaningful Mission statement of our brand 'Make My Fish'. This mission statement needs be used where ever you are introducing your food brand on social media platforms like Google, YouTube, Instagram, and Facebook. This need be used in online and offline marketing to establish the connect with your customers and your food brand.

Step3: Establish brand's online presence: A strong online presence is very essential for business, as any customer before ordering the food, do check online for the reviews of the food offered by the brand. In this digital era, most of the people are addicted to social media platforms like Facebook, YouTube, Instagram. The more often the brand is seen by the customers on these social media platforms, higher are the chances for the prospective customers to memorize your brand name and higher are the chances consumers will order from your brand when they are in the need of the food.

When customers call to place orders for Book My Chicken or any of our other brands, we ask customers how did they get to know about our brand and how did they get the contact number, and customer responds saying, 'On Google, we looked for chicken special / seafood special place in my area and your brand's name appeared first. The reviews were awesome so we wanted to order from this place.' How does that feel? Great, Awesome!!

There are effective strategies you need to follow to get your brand name listed in top search results when people look for special food in your area on social media. That is called branding it right.

1: How to list your brand:

While listing your brand on social media say Google My Business or Facebook, list it with [Brand Name] – Best place in [city/area name] to get [1 USP] [Food niche]

For example: My brands are listed on Google My Business as

Book My Chicken – Best place in Vartak Nagar, Thane West to get homemade chicken dishes.

The Wok Delight – Best place in Vartak Nagar, Thane West for Chinese food.

Make My Fish – Best place in Vartak Nagar, Thane West to get authentic, hygienic, and delicious seafood.

It is most likely that the customers will use the search criteria as 'Best place in [city/area name] to get [USP] [food niche].' So, if these search keywords are already present in your brand's listing information, higher are the chances that your brand will be listed in top search results wherever customers look for it on Google search.

2: Where to list your business:

Essentially, you need to list your business on following **TEN** places where customers are most likely to look for the best food brands before ordering food.

1. **Google My Business:** The most used search engine is Google.com. Google also helps businesses to list their presence online using Google My Business. The google Maps helps to locate the address/location of your

brand. Google reviews help to build the trust in your brand, refer to the food reviews and get more orders.

Look for the tutorial on how to list business on Google My Business and you will find multiple articles which will help you in listing your business on Google. The steps are very easy and it is completely free. It will ask for your brand name, logo, business address, location, type of business/service, Business website (you can provide your food aggregator's link or Facebook page link, if you are not having a dedicated brand's website yet.), business hours details and business mobile number. While configuring the brand name, do follow the template explained earlier so that your brand is highlighted in top searches. Also, while configuring the business description, use the major keywords like your Brand's USPs, your area name, brand name, food niche and 'best' keyword, your target customers (like students/families, bachelors, employees), your special dish names. This helps for Google to highlight your brand in search results when people search using such keywords on Google.

Once you configure all these details step by step as guided on Google My Business, finally it verifies your business (it probably takes 7 to 15 working days to verify your business by Google) and then your brand's Google listing go online/visible.

2. **Trip Advisor:** Like Google, people are most likely checkout the Trip Advisor for the recommendation of

food brands. *https://tripadvisor.com/CreateListing* Refer to this webpage and follow the steps over there to get your brand's listing done on Trip Advisor. It is very easy and completely free. Again, wherever possible like in Brand Name, Brand description, use the major keywords as explained earlier to get your brand highlighted whenever people search online.

3. **JustDial Listing:** It is very important to have your business listed on JustDial. This is also like TripAdvisor Listing. Very easy and completely free. Visit the website *https://justdial.com/Free-Listing* Enter the basic details about your brand name, mobile number and other details as asked. Again, while entering company/brand name, use the major keywords, brand's USPs as explained earlier to get your brand highlighted in top whenever people search online.

4. **Zomato:** Online Food Ordering platform (Aggregator)

Online Food aggregator like Zomato is the place where people generally search for options to look for ordering food online when they are hungry. So, it is obvious to have your food business listed on this platform to get noticed by the customers. The process for listing on these platforms has been made online and is very straight forward. Visit the website *https://www.zomato.com/partner-with-us* (or simply search for Zomato partner on Google to get the latest website by Zomato) and follow the straight forward steps mentioned over there to Register your outlet/brand/restaurant. For registration, the basic details required are FSSAI license copy, PAN card (This can be your individual PAN card or of company's PAN card), Regular GSTIN (if applicable), Bank account details, Your brand's menu items, Dish images of at least 5 items.

FSSAI should be of the location from where you are starting the food business. Initially, you can get the FSSAI done for your home address, till the time you finalize the commercial location for your outlet and proceed with the processing. Once the listing is done, its very easy to get the address updated on FSSAI or go for a new FSSAI for new location. By doing this, you can bypass the time required to get onboarded on Zomato. Initially, you can prepare a sample menu based on the research/survey you have done. Take the sample dish images (images downloaded from internet will not work). And proceed with the Zomato Onboarding process as guided on the website It is simple.

It generally takes 7 to 15 working days to get listed on Zomato platform.

5. **Swiggy :** Online Food Ordering Platform (Aggregator)

Swiggy is another most popular application people use to order food online. It is obvious to have your food business listed on this platform as well to get noticed by the customers and receive the orders. The process for listing on this platform is also straight forward and has been made online. Visit the website *https://partner-with-us.swiggy.com/onboard#/ swiggy* (or simply search for Swiggy partner with us on Google to get the latest website by Swiggy) and follow the straight forward steps mentioned over there to Register your outlet/brand/restaurant. For registration, the basic details required are FSSAI license or FSSAI acknowledgment, PAN card (This can be your individual PAN card or of company's PAN card), GSTIN Certificate (at some places its mandatory), Bank account details (Cancelled Cheque or bank passbook), Your brand's menu items.

Since aggregator onboarding is location specific, follow the same tips given for FSSAI, in the above point for Zomato onboarding. Initially, you can prepare a sample menu based on the research/survey you have done. This can be updated later after onboarding. Take the sample dish images (images downloaded from internet will not work). And proceed with the Swiggy Onboarding process as guided on the website It is quite simple.

It generally takes 7 to 15 working days to get listed on Swiggy platform.

6. **Magicpin Listing:** This is another online food ordering platform where your outlet should be listed on to get noticed by the customers. Check whether Magicpin is operational in your city. To get listed on

this platform, visit *https://magicpin.in/partners/* (or simply do a Google search for Magicpin partner to get the latest link.) Follow the simple steps as guided by the online portal by giving the basic information about your brand, yourself, FSSAI details, bank details, city and complete the process of onboarding. It usually takes 7 to 15 working days to get listed on Magicpin platform.

7. **Instagram:** social media plays crucial role in branding. Instagram is powerful tool used by many people for social media updates. Very important to have your brand's profile/account created on Instagram platform. Simply follow the instructions/steps given for online profile creation on Instagram.com to create your brand specific profile/account.

8. **Facebook:** Another powerful social media platform is Facebook. Its essential to have your brand specific page created on Facebook. The Facebook profile should be of your company name. Under this profile, you can have brand specific Facebook page. If you have multiple brands, then under the same company profile, create multiple Facebook pages. Its very simple to create the Facebook page for your brand. Simply Google search for create Facebook page and you will get a step-by-step guide by Facebook to create the page. Do use the major keywords as explained earlier while adding description of your brand and other places where ever applicable

so that your page gets highlighted in searches when people search for these major keywords.

9. **WhatsApp Business:** This is a powerful tool to get direct orders from customers, to connect with customers personally and to create your custom groups to differentiate customer categories. WhatsApp helps you to connect personally with customer in one to one chat, resolve any queries/issues, update the status on WhatsApp with offer details, menu dishes social media posts, videos, recipe making short videos, customer reviews posts. This helps customers to stay engaged with your brand's activities and updates. This attracts customers for re-ordering with direct orders.

   WhatsApp groups help to keep all the people, who are interested in your brand/food niche together. Have such groups as Admin only to post the regular updates about your menu, offers, festival greetings. Groups can be differentiated based on Order-Done, No-order, Repeat-orders if you want to have different offers based on the category of customers.

10. **YouTube:** YouTube is the most popular social media platform where people are engaged to. Its essential to have your brand specific YouTube channel so that when people search for your brand on Google, your brand's listing on YouTube is displayed in the Top search results. Creating YouTube channel is very easy and is free of cost.

To create YouTube channel, you need to have your brand specific gmail account. Sign-in to YouTube with this gmail account, click on the profile picture and get the option to create a Channel. Follow the process/steps as guided online to complete the YouTube channel creation. Its very easy and straightforward. Simply do a google search for 'Create YouTube channel' and you will get the step-by-step guide by Google Support to help you have your brand specific YouTube channel created.

On this YouTube channel, you can post the introductory videos of your brand, launch of new dishes, recipe making short videos, offers, short videos of your outlet setup, cleanliness maintained at your outlet. This way people will connect more with your brand. As you keep discipline, continuity in posting videos on your brand's YouTube channel, the YouTube subscribers increases on your channel and video play time goes above the time as prescribed by YouTube. Post that you start earning extra passive income from YouTube. Hurry!!

3: Offer extraordinary customer service:

Branding is not only about visuals and messaging on social media. It also involves the customer experience. Have a disciplined and polite approach towards the customers. Train your staff to provide excellent customer service and create an environment that reflects your brand identity.

For our Brands, we have set a process which trains our staff on how to interact with customers over phone, in writing and in person. You need to **reflect the class, ethics/values of your brand while you interact with customers**.

Below are the scenarios where you need to interact with customers. Giving some actual customer reactions while we practiced the same.

1. **Enquiry calls, to give orders:** Customer quoted *'You are so kind and you are talking so genuinely, I will surely visit your outlet and would love to eat from your place.'*

2. To give update on order delivery status.

    Customer quoted *'This is the first time I am getting such call to give an update on order dispatchment. I am overwhelmed and that's so kind of you. What is your name?'*

    Another customer quoted, *'I am highly impressed with the way you talk and took time to update us on the order status. No one does this. I am pretty sure, by continuing doing this, you will take your brand to a whole new level. Best wishes.'*

3. Ask for feedback, revert to positive or negative feedback.

    Customer quoted *'Glad to see the zest for getting the service feedback. Surely you have a long way to go. All the best.'*

4. Written communication asking for feedback.

    Customer quoted *'We were gladly surprised to see a handwritten note along with the parcel. I have still preserved that note with me for future references.'*

5. **Circulate the offers:**

    Customer quoted *'The way you draft the offers is very attention seeker. Your offer posts are attractive. Good branding and promotion. Keep it up.'*

    Can you see, over this communication, the customers are bonding/connecting with you at a personal level. Not only over the food, but they connect with you, as a person, as face of your brand. And that is your big achievement as a food entrepreneur.

4: Participate in local events:

Participating in local events, such as food festivals and society annual gatherings, community gatherings, can help you build your brand and connect with your target audience. It also gives an opportunity to showcase your food offerings, distribute any food samples and get feedback from customers. Record these customer feedback in the form of videos, written communication and post it on social media for larger coverage.

Always remember, branding is an ongoing process. Continuously evaluate and refine your brand to ensure it remains relevant and resonates with your customers.

All secrets revealed! Note down your branding strategy, which places you completed the listing of your brands. This is very crucial activity towards socializing you food business and getting more sales. Pay very high attention to do it right. In the following chapters we will revisit again to these branding places/tools to see how to get more orders.

In the next chapter, we are going to understand the secrets of deciding the menu items and pricing for your brand. Excited?? Let us move forward to launch your cloud kitchen.

CHAPTER 10

SECRET 10:
STRATEGIES TO DECIDE THE MENU ITEMS AND PRICING

'How did you decide on the menu items to sell under your brand?' 'How did you decide on the portions?' 'How to calculate the pricing?'

So many questions, right? Not to worry. In this chapter we will extract all secrets of effective strategies to decide the menu items to sale under your brand and arriving at their pricing. Let us begin.

While deciding the menu and menu items in your chosen food niche, always remember the golden line 'Less is always good'. Instead of having all the possible food items in single menu, have few (less than 10 if you are a new entrant in food business and if this is your first brand.) most popular and in demand menu items as per your target market research. This helps greatly in reducing the inventory cost. In online scenario, with less menu items, it becomes very easy for the target customers to choose quickly from the limited menu to place an order. Later, based on the market response you can modify (add/reduce) the menu items.

The effective strategies that we used and helped us greatly while finalizing our menu items are:

1. **Target market research:** Now that we have decided whom to sell our food, conduct a survey in market (as explained in market research section earlier) to understand the food preferences and needs (how often consumers want to order such food) of your target customers.

    Use the food aggregator's data to check the best seller menu items in your food niche. Use this information to create a menu that serves to your target customers.

2. **Keep it simple, less is more:** Keep the menu simple and easy to navigate, with a few signature dishes that sets your brand apart from competitors. Mark few menu items as best sellers, spicy, medium spicy. Also have people puller menu items (which are always in demand (in your chosen food niche and are available at a lower cost). Example of this: For a fast-food niche, have the people puller items like Vadapav, Dabeli at a standard market price or may be little lower price than market. For a Chinese brand, have the people puller / always in demand items like veg Manchurian or chilli chicken at a standard market price or little lower. For a Thali specific brand, have a basic (mini) Thali available at a minimal cost for the people to try out food from your

brand. More menu items result in high inventory cost and food wastage. A smaller menu helps with inventory management and reduces food waste.

3. **Calculate food costs and profit margins:** From the best seller food items in your chosen niche, check the cost of all ingredients and calculate total cost of recipe. Determine how many portions you need to sell for each menu item to make a profit. Now, use this information to set competitive prices while ensuring profitability.

   For example, calculate the cost of all ingredients to prepare Chicken Kolhapuri Masala from 1KG chicken. Calculate how many saleable portions can be made available from 1KG chicken. With per plate 4 chicken pieces, 5 plates chicken kolhapuri masala is the saleable portion for which we need to decide the pricing to ensure profitability. The pricing should not be too high than the competitors pricing or should not be very low than the market price.

4. **Offer portion sizes and combos:** Now that we have finalized our menu items (less than 10 if you are starting new and this is your first brand), offer a variety in terms of portion size (such as one plate, Half Handi, Full Handi or portions like Small, Medium and Large) to cater to different requirements of your target customers. This helps to create lucrative offers for one portion size which customers will go for to try out

your products. Gradually, they get upgraded to higher portions.

With limited menu items, have variations by forming combos of the related menu items. Example: Chicken one plate with Chapatis and Rice. Fried Momos with Soup, Chicken Noodles with Soup. This helps to give more value to customers at lower costs. Using the same inventory, we can have variations in terms of combos.

5. **Use pricing psychology:** Use pricing strategies such as odd pricing (e.g., 99/- instead of 100/-) and anchor pricing (e.g., highlighting the most expensive item on the menu to make other items pricing seem more reasonable). Never have the menu items arranged in lower to higher or higher to lower pricing sequence, but have mix order. Higher priced items followed by lowest followed by middle lower prices. This way customer mind does not focus more on pricing details but on the menu items that they would be interested to purchase.

Menu items which have variations in terms of portion size such as Half, Full, or Small, Medium and Large always use the pricing psychology to make the customers feel the smaller portion looks costly than the higher variation of the same. Thus, forcing customer to go for higher portion as it gives more value with smaller increment in pricing.

For example, Chicken Noodles Half (139/-) and Full (169/-) Obviously, the customer will be happy to pay

40/- extra to get Full portion of Chicken Noodles. This pricing psychology helps to migrate the customers to higher portion menu items thus increasing the profitability as for you the Food cost is more or less same for either portions.

Another effective pricing strategy is to highlight the cost /prices in smaller text sizes. It is human phycology that whichever is in small size is interpreted as less whereas whichever is highlighted in bigger size/bold font is interpreted as high cost. While projecting cost of your menu item on offer posts, menu cards, posters/ flexes always highlight the cost in smaller text size for the end customer to perceive it as less cost.

6. **Learn from Market:** Monitor sales and adjust as needed: Regularly monitor sales data to identify in-demand and no-demand menu items. Finally, it is the market / target customers who will respond to the menu items launched. Use this information to adjust your menu and pricing accordingly.

7. **Continuous Market Research to stay on top of food trends:** Keep watch with food trends in the market and incorporate them into your menu to attract customers who are interested in trying new things.

8. **Get feedback and learn from the feedback:** Encourage your customers to provide feedback on the menu and pricing. Incorporate this feedback to make

improvements and adjustments to meet customer expectations.

So, got the ideas on designing an effective menu with saleable food items! Work out on the portions, combos, and their competitive prices. Get the menu designed from a professional menu designer. You can do it yourself using Canva tool, but I recommend to get this done professionally by the people who are expert at it. You have lot more things to focus on as an entrepreneur.

Having decided the menu, what next? How do we pack it? Customers will perceive your brand value based on their first look at the food parcel received from you! Are you getting the importance of packaging? Want to know the secrets and the strategies of effective packaging? Then let us begin our next chapter. Stay focused!

CHAPTER 11

SECRET 11: PACK IT PERFECT! STRATEGIES FOR EFFECTIVE PACKAGING

'Your packaging is very sturdy and effective.' 'Very professional way of packing food items. I was very much impressed with your packaging.' 'When we received the food parcel, we got a feel of five-star brand. Keep it up!'

Wow and Fantastic feeling, right? What more a happy food entrepreneur can expect!

Once you finalize on the menu items to sell, as per the chosen niche, the next obvious task is to consider the right strategies for its effective packaging. In cloud kitchen where major focus is on food delivery, for the customers, packaging of parcel as received is the first and last impression of your brand even before customer opens the parcel and tastes your food. Therefore, effective packaging plays a major role in how customers perceive your brand. Eventually people don't just buy food, they buy brand. Even though you are running your cloud kitchen from home, customers should get a feel as if the food has been received from a five-star brand.

Below are the secrets that you should know while finalizing the packaging.

1. **Keep the packaging simple and functional:** The packaging should be easy to use, to handle, to transport and to store. It should also protect the food inside from damage or spoilage. It should also prevent any food leakages.

2. **Use high-quality materials:** In case of cloud kitchen scenario, your brand value is going to be perceived based on your packaging. Do not compromise on the quality. The packaging materials should be of good quality, durable, safe, and eco-friendly. The poor- or low-quality material will lead to bad handling of food, food leakages and eventually leads to bad impression on customers.

3. **Branding and labelling:** Consider the menu items portion sizes to finalize on the sizes of the related packaging boxes. The branding design should be consistent across all the packaging boxes. Branding design should highlight the basic details such as brand name, call or WhatsApp number of your outlet, location of your outlet. Get these branding details printed on the labels/stickers which need to go across all the packaging boxes, in all portion sizes.

4. **Convenience:** The packaging should be convenient to open, serve, and dispose of. The portion sizes should also be appropriate for the menu items and target audience and for the desired costing of menu items. Packaging should be different for different food niche.

5. **Sustainability:** The packaging should be recyclable, biodegradable, or compostable to reduce the environmental impact. Also check for the local state government rules for allowed or not-allowed types of packaging materials to avoid any penalty on outlet.

6. **Customization:** Customizing the packaging according to food item types and according to seasonal needs can create a unique selling proposition for the product. For example, to prevent any spoilage of packaging or food during rainy season, instead of using the paper cover bags, use the plastic (as allowed by the government guidelines) cover bags.

7. **Cost-effective:** The packaging should also be cost-effective without compromising the quality and safety of the food items. Reducing the amount of packaging material can help to reduce the costs. Consider your target market such as premium customers, students, middle class customers for finalizing the cost of your suitable packaging.

Having discussed about effective strategies to finalize on the packaging, let us also check the important points while purchasing the packaging material. These are the pearls of wisdom, so pay attention!

Where from and how much packaging material to purchase:

Online Purchase:

In the world of digitization, the packaging material is also available to purchase online. Checkout the leading shopping websites *http://indiamart.com* and *https://www.amazon.com/* for the varieties of packaging material available. Also visit *https://www.gujaratshopee.com/* for the latest packaging materials for various types of food items. Use the right strategies as explained earlier to finalize the packaging material suitable to the food items.

Offline Purchase:

In your city/locality checkout the market place to get the packaging material in wholesale rates. Connect with other outlets/restaurants to check out from where do they purchase the packaging materials. Get the contact details of the vendors supplying the packaging material and tie-up with them for the regular purchases. Negotiate for the best rates possible. Most of these vendors provide door-step delivery to the outlet.

Most of the packaging vendors, in both online/ offline purchases, provide **sample kits** of your chosen packaging.

Get the sample kits first and try out various packaging options for the suitability for the specific food item, do the basic testing for any leakages, food temperature, handling and movement. This helps greatly in finalizing the packaging. Almost all the packaging vendors, in both online and offline purchases, offer discounted rates provided you purchase in bulk quantity. However, before falling for the lucrative rates on bulk purchases such as purchasing minimum quantity of 4000 or 10000 units, do take your budget into consideration. Otherwise, such bulk purchases results into dead investments and major chunk of money remains invested in packaging material. Once the outlet is launched and is in operation, based on the monthly rolling of the orders, you can always go for bulk or need basis purchasing of packaging material. This is the wise approach we followed.

Huh! So many secrets and peals of wisdom! With so much of knowledge, list down which packaging material will you use for the food items in your menu. List down the vendors from whom will you make these purchases. With this, a major step is completed towards building and launching your cloud kitchen! Congratulations!

Now the million-dollar question for you. Who will do the cooking? Ha-ha. Whether you know the cooking or not, we have secrets for all! Nothing to worry. Just read through the next chapter to know the secrets of Chef-less model!

CHAPTER 12

SECRET 12: WHO WILL DO THE COOKING? EFFECTIVE STRATEGIES FOR CHEF LESS MODEL.

'Very delicious and tasty food.' 'OMG, such a homely taste.' 'This is my 7th order with Book My Chicken. Very authentic taste and consistency in the taste and quality. Keep it up team.' 'As always, the food was awesome. Everything was just perfect. My guests enjoyed it.'

If you are a cook, personally, how satisfied and proud you feel with these review remarks from your customers! Paid off all the efforts of converting my passion for cooking food and serving to the society when we got such actual reviews from our customers, again and again. Even if you are not a cook, but your team is delivering such work, how proud you feel to get into food entrepreneurship.

The secret here is to maintain the consistency in taste and quality to retain your customers. In this chapter, let us elaborate more and dig into the complete secret to get the wider understanding.

In earlier chapters, we have covered all the major secrets of building and launching your first food brand, now the most important factor is about who will do the cooking? Without this the cloud kitchen operation is incomplete. There are two answers to this, With Chef or No Chef (chef less). Let us see the effective strategies for both.

Cooking With Chef:

Cooking with a chef involves working with a professional culinary expert who has formal educational background of a well-known hotel management degree, who has the knowledge and experience to create delicious, restaurant-quality meals. Here are some effective strategies to keep in mind when cooking with a chef:

1. **Trust their expertise:** Chefs have years of experience and training, so trust their knowledge and skills.

2. **Learn new techniques:** Take advantage of the opportunity to learn new techniques and skills from a chef. Ask questions and observe their methods.

3. **Prep ahead of time:** Chefs typically prep all their ingredients before cooking. To keep up, take their guidance on which ingredients to prepare ahead of time.

4. **A clean and organized kitchen:** A clean and organized kitchen is essential for efficient cooking.

Follow the chef's lead in keeping the kitchen clean and organized.

5. **Taste often:** Tasting your food throughout the cooking process is crucial to ensure proper seasoning and flavour.

6. **Make it a joyful journey:** Cooking with a chef can be a fun and educational experience. Enjoy the process and learn as much as you can.

7. **Finalize the scope of work with chef:** Beforehand, work with the chef and finalize how many recipes the chef will provide you out of your brand's menu. Some of the professional chef, charge you based on number of recipes to provide you with whereas few professionals work based on entire menu of the brand. Accordingly, they charge their cost to you. Have a clarity on this before onboarding a professional chef.

8. **Finalize the association period with chef:** Have a clarity on how long you want the chef to be associated with your brand. Association period can be contact basis, such as onboard the chef for three months (for example). During this period, finalize with him on your desired niche specific recipes and then the chef handovers these recipes to you, trains the fellow staff members and yourself on these recipes and then gets disassociated from your brand and moves on. Few of the professional chef work on such contract basis model. Have a clear understanding on this to finalize

the association period with chef. The long term engagement of Chef with your brand may prove to be a costly affaire considering their costing. So do have check on your budget before onboarding the chef.

9. **Documenting the recipes and training:** Mutually agree on the work output from the chef before getting the chef onboarded. The chef should agree to give the final recipe of the food items in written documents and videos for future references. Also agree on training the junior staff member/s and yourself on the final recipes. This helps in minimizing the risk of becoming dependant on one person to run your outlet's operations in long run. Never be dependant on single person (cook/chef) if you want to succeed in your cloud kitchen business.

   Even though you appoint a chef / cook to run the outlet's main operation of cooking, the top priority point is to train yourself in all the recipes of the food items related to your brand. You as a owner need to know what ingredients and in which proportion they are required, what is the step by step method to prepare the recipes. This way you will not be taken on a ride by your staff for the inventory management and no one can blackmail you to run your outlet's cooking operation. Thus, reducing the people dependency.

Cooking without Chef and going Chef-Less:

Most of the people who get into the cloud kitchen business are the ones who are passionate about food or cooking. You also planned and got into this business to pursue your passion of cooking or love for food. This is a great foundation to start your cloud kitchen brand's cooking operation without Chef.

The secrets behind the right strategies to adapt when you are going Chef-Less are:

a. **Self-Learn when you know cooking on your own:** If you already know how to cook, that is a great advantage. You will need to learn few basics about how to portion your recipe as per the costing decided, how to do food presentation post it is ready to pack, how to do topping/seasoning and what other side cutlery (example spoon, paper napkin, sauces sachet, pickle sachet, salt sachet depending on your brand's niche) to go along with the main dish. You will learn this by observing how other outlets in the similar niche serve you the similar food item. This should be covered in your research part when you are finalizing the menu items.

b. **Self-learn when you do not know cooking:** Even though you don't know cooking, you decided to start the cloud kitchen for the love of food. So, your first step is to learn cooking the dishes that you finalized to sale. The effective strategy to learn quickly are:

1. **Research and finalize for recipes:** Look for the recipe books, YouTube videos and Websites having the detailed description of recipes along with the list of ingredients. There are lots of

famous chefs YouTube channels available where they showcase the recipes in details. Check which recipe suits you for ease of understanding, ease of preparation and tastes good. After research using these resources, finalize at least three recipes for your food item. For each of the three recipes, prepare the dish two times following the same preparation steps to ensure the result / food items comes out the same and in same quantity. After each preparation, have the dish tasted by your family members/neighbours or friends and take the feedback for improvements, suggestions. Basis that do any alterations to the recipe and have the final testing done. Follow these steps for each shortlisted recipe of a specific dish and finalize on one basis tasting feedback. Have the final recipe documented for further references.

By Self learn and cooking by self, we do not intend to become cook for a long run and be occupied in the cooking operations for long. However, we need to self-learn and be hands on the cooking so that when you hire a cook or junior staff, they do not blackmail you. You do not become dependent on the staff and will always be confident on running your business on your own shoulders. Your foundation of your business become strong.

c. **Use Readymade products:** The products like gravy pre-mixes, various masala mixes, Frozen items are very handy in terms of saving on time, labour cost, food wastage and ease of preparations. In case of bulk orders, these readymade products come very handy in quick preparations and delivery. Readymade deserts like Gulab Jamun helps in saving on preparation time, labour cost and ease of handling. Example of masala mixes are Biryani Mix, Chole Mix, Kebab masala mix, Tandoori Masala mix. Examples of frozen food items are Fish Fingers, Burger Patty, Samosa, Fries, Momos. Have a quality and taste check done before finalizing on the specific brand of these readymade products. Some of the most popular brands providing such readymade premixes are Regal Kitchen Foods, Karamat, Cremica and APRIL3RDFOOD

d. **Tie-up with local vendors to get ready made food items:** Its always good idea to get ready made food items like chapatis, parathas, desserts (like Gulab Jamun), cold beverages like Solkadhi, Cold-drinks outsourced to small local vendors. This way we save on lot of efforts and time to prepare such items in-house. The cost of preparation of these items comes almost equal to the cost in which you get it from the local vendors on regular basis.

e. **Take help from close ones:** If you do not know cooking but your close ones like your mother, sister, brother, husband/wife, relatives know the cooking and are ready to work with you to assist in the business, then take their help. This also works well in initial stage to start off. However, we need to get the junior staff to assist and scale up further in the business.

In all the scenarios we talked above for chef less model, the important point is to build the proper system, document the recipes and train the junior staff as well as yourself. Creating systems and documenting recipes helps to prepare the dish consistently in same manner and ensuring the product turns out to be the same irrespective of who is preparing it. This is how the outlet goes Chef-less in long run. The well-known brands such as McDonald, KFC, operates on chef-less models as they standardise their recipes and document it, train their staff on these recipes and produce the same end products. **Building proper systems** for your outlet's operations helps you, as an owner, to get freed from the cooking operation of the outlet and focus on other important aspects of business-like marketing, hiring, and scaling up.

Huh! Got a relief with all the secrets opened to you! Relax, you can do it!

In the next chapter, we will cover how much staff is required? From where to hire the staff and what are the secrets behind hiring right staff? Let us dive-in.

CHAPTER 13

SECRET 13: STRATEGIES TO HIRE RIGHT STAFF – HOW MUCH STAFF IS NEEDED AND FROM WHERE TO HIRE THEM?

'How much staff do you have at your outlet? How many people do we really need to run the cloud kitchen? From where can I get the staff? I am a cook myself, so do I need staff to run my business?'

So many questions around staffing and hiring. Just chill. We have answers to all. The secret is getting unfolded. Pay attention.

You are into food business for the love and passion for the food/cooking. Naturally, you tend to pursue your passion of cooking by starting the cloud kitchen operations by self-cooking. But as the business grows, as a owner you need to look after all the aspects of business like operations, marketing, hiring, you cannot keep doing cooking for longer or continuously throughout the business life. We need to hire staff, train them, and get the day-to-day operations being handled by them.

I started my cloud kitchen first two brands with Self cooking mode. For the initial good two years I was doing self-cooking and realized that although I enjoy it, if we need to grow the business and scale it up, We need to focus on other aspects like marketing, branding. For doing so, your mind needs to be free from the kitchen work. Otherwise, physically, and mentally you feel exhausted in day-to-day operations of business and cannot focus on scaling up and growth of the business. That is the reason you need to hire staff, train them, and delegate the tasks. Otherwise, the business becomes a one-man-army solution and you become a single point of failure. If you are unwell or out of town for some work/family function your business stops. Hiring team/staff and delegating the tasks that you have been doing single handily is the only way forward to grow and scale up your food business. It is very important for you as an owner to get free from business to think and grow your business more. To grow further, you need to be working from outside the business not from inside the business. If you stay inside the business, you become a worker not an entrepreneur. That is the key secret revealed.

In this chapter, we will elaborate on:

1. Minimum staff requirements for a cloud kitchen

2. From where to hire staff

3. How to hire right staff.

Let us begin with how much minimum staff is required:

When you are a new entrant in the food business and this is your first brand, you would need minimum four people with following role and responsibilities:

1. **Cook:** If you are a good cook and you have finalized on the recipes of your menu items of your brand, you need a cook who can follow your recipes and do the food preparations and order executions.

   If you do not know cooking and the recipes of your menu items need to be finalized for which you need assistance/help, then you would need a Chef/cook who knows the in and out of the recipes in your chosen niche.

   Hire a chef to finalize the recipes with proper food tasting. If you have a limited budget, then hire a chef on contract basis (for 3 months) with an agreement to **finalize menu items and their recipes** for your brand. Have these recipes documented with videos to train the other junior staff and for your reference in future. The cook/chef should be able to **train the junior staff** to ramp them up on recipes and order preparation. Cook/Chef should help you to **standardize the cooking operations**. By standardization we mean, the menu item should be prepared using same ingredients, should have same texture, same taste, same portion size, same quality. Customers want consistency. The consistency comes by standardization of recipes and operations.

Whoever is preparing the menu items by following this standardized recipe and method, the output must be same. Major responsibility with cook/chef is to **reduce KPT (Kitchen Performance Time)**. Cook/Chef needs to ensure the food preparation time is as low as possible so that orders can be made ready with minimum food preparation time. Food preparation time is a major criteria customer looks for before placing orders to an outlet. The cook/chef should work continuously to keep the KPT as low as possible without compromising on the quality. This can be achieved by doing pre-preparation of masalas, gravies, pre-cooked supporting items.

Do NOT hire a cook/Chef for:

a. **To decide Brand's food niche:** Which type of food to sale, what should be the niche of your brand? This decision needs to be taken by you (by doing the market survey and other strategies that we talked about in earlier chapters.) and NOT by the cool/chef (they will go by what they know to cook without considering what is the demand of your target market.)

b. **To setup and launch your food business:** Don't be dependant on the cook/chef to get your food business setup done. This should be your sole responsibility to define and setup your food brands as the way market demands and you want.

c. **To decide the Menu and Price:** Which menu items should be offered by your brand should be decided by you by doing the research and target market's preference as elaborated in the earlier chapters. The pricing need to be derived based on the ingredients used, quantity used, raw material cost, preparation cost. Deriving the costing of the finalized menu items should be your responsibility, the cook/chef can help you by listing the ingredients used in the recipes.

d. **To increase the sale:** Cook/Chef is NOT responsible to increase the sale of the outlet. It is completely your / sales manager's responsibility to focus on marketing and sales growth of the food outlet. Cook/Chef are responsible to cater to the increased orders by doing proper inventory managements and quick food preparation.

e. **To have the menu as per cook/chef's know how:** To let the chef/cook decide what should be the menu items based on what he/she knows to cook. This is a big NO. If you let the cook/chef to control the menu of your food brand based on what he/she knows, the foundation of your food brand is too shaky and is at High Risk. If the cook/chef leaves you, your business collapses immediately.

2. **Supervisor / Manager:** A supervisor or a manager is required at the outlet to help you in following activities:

a. **Hiring:** Manager should assist or help you to hire other staff members required for the outlet.

b. To ensure team/staff is following the standardised recipes, systems, and **day to day operations** of the outlet are happening smoothly.

c. To coordinate for receiving orders, dispatching orders, to handle Take Aways and to handle Delivery boys. The manager should be responsible for co-ordinating for receiving orders via multiple sources: direct orders via phone/WhatsApp or website or via food aggregator platforms like Zomato and Swiggy. Coordinate with cook/staff for getting the order ready in stipulated time and ensuring the timely dispatching of the order via delivery boys or to the customers visiting the outlet for Takeaways. In case of direct orders, manager should ensure delivery boys are arranged for the order pickup and ensure their payments and timely delivery of the food parcel to the customers.

d. **To manage complaints:** Supervisor or manager should be capable to handle or manage the customer complaints received about the orders. The complaint management can be via oral communication (over phone/WhatsApp) or written communication (over online portals of food delivery aggregators, Google My Business) with customers. Manager should also look into and resolves any complaints regarding delivery boys, delayed delivery of orders.

e. **To assist in marketing:** Manager should assist you in implementing your marketing plans. The ownership of deciding the marketing strategy remains with you. Manager can assist you in implementing the marketing plans. It can be local area marketing, online marketing or handling the social media accounts of your brand.

Do NOT hire a manager for following expectations:

1. **To handle full business:** Do not hire a supervisor/manager thinking that he/she will handle your full food business. The business has to be controlled by you. Manager will assist you in the operational tasks as we discussed above.

2. **To control the staff:** Do not have expectation that the manager will control the staff of the outlet. The staff/team management need to be done by you as a owner. This need to be achieved by conducting business and operational meetings regularly (daily, once in fifteen days and once in a month) to take reviews, feedbacks and further growth plans. The appraisals of the staff need to be done by you as owner. Manager can share his/her inputs.

3. **To create the systems of operations:** Do not expect the manager/supervisor to create the systems of operations for your outlet. This need be done by you

considering the brand's vision and quality that you expect from your brand.

4. **To create Vision/Goal of your brand:** Do not expect the manager or supervisor to create the vision or Goal of your brand. Your food business/brand is your baby. No other person can create or understand your vision or goal of starting this business. Defining the Goal and Vision of your brand is your sole responsibility.

5. **To set yourself free from business:** Do not expect that you will be completely free from business by appointing a manager or supervisor. You need to work from outside of the business to grow and scale it up further. The manager and staff are to help you achieve this. They will help you to manage the day to day operations of the outlet and allow you to focus on other aspects of the business like marking and sales.

3. **Kitchen Helper:** Helper is required to take care of inventory. Raw material management, organising and tracking the stock, vegetables, cleaning of non-veg items (meat, chicken, and fish). Helper also works along with cook and assists him in recipe preparation by cutting vegetables, non-veg items. Helper also works to co-ordinate to get the inventory from market. Helper also assists to deliver the food parcel in nearby areas. You will have to set these work expectations with staff to avoid any miscommunications. We had also set the expectations for a kitchen helper that he/she should

know the cooking and should learn from and ramp up with cook to prepare the menu items recipes. The helper should have interest in cooking. So that they can prepare food as per order in case cook is on leave. This way you can set the expectations and way forward for the growth of the helper in your organization.

4. **Kitchen Cleaner:** Cleaner is required to take care of the daily cleaning of kitchen, daily cleaning of utensils, deep cleaning of kitchen on weekly and monthly basis, periodic maintenance, or deep cleaning of major equipment in kitchen such as deep freezer, Refrigerator, Microwave, Oven, Kitchen Chimney, Burners. Cleaner should also be considered for the delivery of the food parcel in nearby areas. Cleaner should be ramped up to scale up to helper's role in long term. Set the expectations with cleaner to take care of the Kitchen Helper's tasks in their absence/leave period. This way you can set the expectations and way forward for the growth of the cleaner in your organization.

From where to hire staff:

Let us see now from where to get/hire staff. Always remember the fact that you will NOT find good staff easily. Hire the team/staff members with right attitude and train them into your culture to make a good team. We have to invest continuously in the people/team in terms of bonding, work ethics, systems and work culture in the outlet. Then only a good team is built. Let us see the places from where we can hire or look for right candidates for food industry.

1. Workindia.in

2. Apana.com

3. OLX

4. Cookfinders.com

5. Hoteljobber.com

These are some of the websites where we can look for the jobseekers in the food industry. Most of these jobseeker's portals provide basic membership (Free/Paid) for the Employers to search for the right candidates. Create the job openings according to your requirements such as job opening for Cook /Chef, Supervisor/Manager and Kitchen Helper on these portals. You will start receiving the job seeker's profiles/calls for these openings. Have a brief discussion with the candidates and call them for a job interview and continue with the hiring process.

6. **Justdial.com:** Make a call on 8888888888 and enquire about the hiring agencies in your area. Get the contact details of the agencies and connect with them for your staffing requirements. However, be careful with the reliability, terms and conditions of these agencies before doing tie-up with them. Have a clarity on their charges before proceeding.

7. **Local Food Businesses:** Connect with the local food businesses and talk to the owner/manager/head-chef to give references of their acquaintances/fellow workers. Many workers from the food industry are in contact with them to seek a job. Be honest and transparent while talking to the local businesses for staff references. Do NOT try to porch their staff. That is not ethical and such staff will not stay with you for longer.

8. **Facebook groups:** On Facebook.com, there are various groups related to hotel industry staffing (Cooks and Chefs and Helpers.) Join such groups in your area/city and post the job opening requirements with all the required details and contact number.

Key points to consider while hiring right staff:

1. **Right Attitude:** For all the positions or staff requirement the most important point to check is the right attitude of the candidate. Even though the candidate is of lesser experience but has great attitude/ethics, he /she can be trained on the required duties. Such staff members will stay with you for longer time. The attitude of the candidate can be checked by asking smart questions (you will find such questions on Google.com) like

   a. 'In your past work experience, did you commit any mistake? How did you rectify such mistakes?'

b. 'If your supervisor shouts on you for something not done rightly, how would you react to it?'

c. 'If you have been told to do certain things in specific way, but you know a better way of doing it, how would you approach this situation?'

d. 'If you see a mischief happening around you, may be by other staff member or your supervisor, what would you do?'

e. 'If there is a bulk order which requires you to work off-duty hours, will you work? How would you handle such orders?'

These are examples of some smart questions which helped us in hiring staff with right attitude based on how they responded to these questions. Based on the role, you can add different questions to check their capabilities and attitude.

2. **Work experience:** Check the prior work experience in the area of work of the candidate. If you are new entrant in food industry, do NOT go for higher experience candidates as they would demand high pay/salary. Lesser work experience candidates would come in the salary range of your budget. However, do check on their work expertise based on the role and their attitude and do not compromise on the quality of work against the salary factor.

3. **Trial and Testing:** For the roles like Cook and Chef, it is must to get the trial and testing done in your outlet by asking the candidate to prepare basic/specific dish from the menu to check their expertise, food taste and speed of preparations. Basis the recipe trial and testing only proceed with the discussion about salary.

4. **Salary:** This is the most crucial deciding factor for you as well as the candidate to accept the job. You need to decide your budget beforehand for the specific roles. Basis the candidate's performance in interview, trials, prior work experience, what they already know/what needs to be trained, you need to arrive at a specific salary for the given role/candidate. Also ensure this salary is competitive as per the current market salary range.

Salary range is dependent on your city, experience level of the candidate and how did they perform in the interview and trial sessions with you. As a reference guideline of salary ranges for the minimum staff requirements for your outlet refer below table: (Pls note, this data is only for the reference and it is always advisable to check in your city and local outlets to ensure the salary ranges.)

Role	Tier 1 City (Metro)	Tier 2 City	Tier 3 City
Cook	Rs 18000/- to Rs 22000/-	Rs 15000/- to Rs 20000/-	Rs 8000/- to Rs 15000/-
Kitchen Helper	Rs 12000/- to Rs 18000/-	Rs 10000/- to Rs 15000/-	Rs 6000/- to Rs 12000/-
Kitchen Cleaner	Rs 8000/- to Rs 11000/-	Rs 6000/- to Rs 10000/-	Rs 3000/- to Rs 6000/-

These salary ranges are from lower side to higher side. Salary ranges get revised time to time. Hence, it is advisable to check in your surrounding areas outlets about what salary range they are offering to their staff.

Feeling very much relaxed now? I heard you saying YES! Now, list down all the activities that you need to do to run your cloud kitchen. Assign the above roles against the activities and start hiring. You will surely build a great team! All the best! Always remember, hiring is a continuous process. So, keep hiring.

Now it is time to plan on next crucial activity of cloud kitchen, that is, food delivery. How do we manage an effective food delivery? What are the secrets behind it to get high customer satisfaction? Let us unveil all the secrets.

CHAPTER 14

SECRET 14: EFFECTIVE STRATEGIES TO MANAGE FOOD DELIVERY

'Thank you for the timely delivery.' 'Food received hot, thank you for the on-time delivery.'

This is what we really want to get the reviews, right? Gives a great sense of fulfilment as an entrepreneur! To achieve this, you need to have effective strategies to manage the food delivery. In this chapter, I will tell real secrets of how to manage food delivery effectively. These are hard earned secrets from own experiences. Real pearls of wisdom. Grab it!

Effective Food Delivery is very important and critical parameter in food business. Especially in cloud kitchen setup where the customers are ordering food online, they would expect the food to be delivered withing 15/20 mins time. As the minimum food preparation time is very important parameter for the customer, the faster delivery time is another parameter for the customer's to consider ordering from your outlet.

'Food was delivered on time', *'Quick delivery and food was received hot.'* These are few of the review comments from our regular customers. These reviews are for the service your outlet is offering to customers. The reviews related to food quality and quantity are related to your outlet's products. It is very important to perform excellently in products and services provided to customers to retain the customers with your brand. Either of this goes wrong, customer satisfaction goes down badly and eventually you loose out on the customer. Hence please pay attention to effectively manage the food delivery in the best possible time expectation, as set with the customers.

Let us understand the secrets of effective strategies to manage the food delivery:

1. For the regular, repeat customers, request them to place the order well in advance (prior one day or minimum 1 hr before.) This helps you to arrange for a delivery partner who can deliver the food parcel.

2. If the delivery location of the customer is far away (beyond 4 km area) from your outlet then set the delivery time expectations accordingly with the customer to agree mutually on the same. Do consider the traffic / road conditions for anticipating the delivery time.

3. When you are a new entrant in food business and are getting daily ten or more orders (min order value of Rs 200/-), then it is good option to hire your own delivery boy to manage the deliveries. However, if the number

of orders per day are lesser, then DO NOT rush to hire your own delivery boy as of now. Work towards getting more and more direct orders and when the order volume goes above 10 per day consistently, then hire your own delivery boy to manage the deliveries effectively. Till then, you can have the Kitchen Helper /Cleaner staff to manage the nearby deliveries (within 2 km area.)

4. Get the delivery done via 3rd party delivery services:

In the market, there are many agencies providing the same day, within 1 hr delivery services including food delivery. In your city, in your locality check out for such third-party delivery services and tie-up with them to get your food delivered. These third-party delivery services are professional service providers and have dedicated people doing only delivery work. Utilize these services to arrange for the delivery to customer's delivery location. Most used Third-Party delivery service providers are Borzo (formerly known as WeFast), Porter, Dunzo, Swiggygiene, ShadowFax. Checkout the availability of these service providers in your area/city and tie up with them. Most of them have easy to use user interface/mobile application to book the delivery partner and specify the pick-up and drop locations. Based on distance between pick-up and drop location, these service providers charge you for the delivery service. These delivery charges you can share along with the customers. Anyways, the food aggregator platforms like (Zomato, Swiggy) also take delivery charges and taxes from customers and you also end up paying the heavy commissions to these food aggregators, you can agree with customers to share 50-50% delivery charges in case delivery charges are too high depending on the distance. In most of the scenarios, customers agree to pay the extra delivery charges. Based on the delivery distance, you can decide whether you can provide FREE Delivery (like within 2 KM area FREE DELIVRY) or based on order value you can provide FREE Delivery (like on orders above Rs 1000/- FREE DELIVERY) offers. This also works to increase the order value as most of the customers do not mind paying for food rather than paying for delivery service.

5. Get the delivery done via Delivery boys of third-party delivery services.

As elaborated in point no 4, as you use third-party Delivery Services and you book their services to deliver food to the customers, their delivery boys visit your outlet for pickup. Most of the delivery boys are willing to take direct orders of delivery work from you, rather than paying commission to the third-party services. Check with these delivery boys for their availability for delivery work for your orders and you pay them per order basis depending on the number of kilometre distance between your outlet and delivery location.

This way delivery boys and you save on the commission the third-party delivery services takes. This is mutually beneficial. Most of the delivery boys agree for this extra income. Do check their area of residence and how soon they can reach to your outlet as you inform them about an order delivery task 30 mins prior to expected time of delivery.

6. Train the supervisor/manager for effective delivery experience to the customers:

Whether you have your own delivery boy or use third party delivery services or their delivery boys to delivery the food order to end customer, until the food is delivered to the customer it is your outlet's sole responsibility of ensuring a smooth delivery experience to your customers. Hence it's very important to train your supervisor or manager on effective management of delivery by coordinating with kitchen operation staff (cook/helper) and delivery staff. Here are the key secret points the manager/supervisor needs to be trained on:

1. Ensure the order getting delivered covers all the food items, side dishes, cutlery as asked by the customers.

2. Ensure the delivery boy (whether your own staff, or any other delivery boy) has been booked well in advance and is available at the outlet at the time of agreed order dispatching time with customer. This requires co-ordination with third party delivery

service (Apps), getting delivery partner assigned, calling up the delivery partner and ensuring he is arriving on time to your outlet.

3. Ensure timely updates are provided to the customers on the status of order like order is ready for dispatching, order has been dispatched via delivery boy. This way customer is updated on the status and appreciate the service.

4. Track the delivery boys and ensure they have reached the delivery location and handed over the order to customers. This requires live tracking of delivery boy location (this facility is mostly available in all the third-party delivery service's apps.) or calling up the delivery partner and checking on his whereabouts.

5. Clearing the payment of the delivery boys : As agreed with the direct delivery boy or via third party delivery service, clear off their payment per order basis. The manager/supervisor should also ensure the customer has been charged appropriately for the delivery service as agreed (Free delivery, 50-50% or 100%) in the total bill to the customer.

6. Customer complaint handling: Even after having all the strategies in place for an effective and hazardless delivery experience to customers, there are chances that the customer complains about the inefficient delivery service in case there

is delay in delivery time (due to heavy traffic, vehicle breakdown issue etc.) or food items got leaked/spoiled during the travel. The supervisor or manager should be trained enough for an effective communication with the customer to ensure the refunds are provided (as appropriate) or give an regular/timely update of delay in expected delivery time (in case of heavy traffic/vehicle breakdown.) This minimises the risk of bad reviews from customers or the risk of loosing out on the customer.

Wow! Those are so cool secret strategies. Isn't it? How many of you got the ideas and got the bulb ON? Now it looks so easy to deliver the food parcels effectively. So, get started! You are ready to launch your food brand! Congratulations!

CHAPTER 15

SECRET 15: STRATEGIES TO GROW FOOD BUSINESS USING AGGREGATOR PLATFORMS

In earlier chapter, we have elaborated on places where you need to list your food business to get noticed by majority of the target audience. One of the most desired listings is on popular food aggregator platforms like Swiggy and Zomato. Magicpin is also another aggregator platform where you can register your food business and get listed. Getting listed on these food aggregator platforms is only one step. After the listing goes live, the next important step is how to grow the orders and grow the food business on aggregator platforms. In this chapter let us dive-in deeper:

Following are the secrets of essential strategies to grow the orders/business on the major aggregator platforms available in your city.

1. **Menu and Food photographs on the aggregator platforms:**

    Always have a simple to browse and small menu listed on the aggregator platforms. In online scenario, customers get confused with a lengthy menu with multiple categories and menu items. **Less is more!** More the menu is short and crispy, more it is understandable by the customer and chances of picking one menu item to order are high when customer is browsing through your outlet's menu.

1. Always have lesser categories/sub-categories and menu items as appropriate to reflect what food (based on your outlet's niche) is available to order from.

2. Ensure for each menu items listed, the appropriate item description highlighting the major ingredients/style of preparations/taste and portion size is provided. This helps the customer to have the clarity about what and how much quantity of food will be delivered to him in the given price. This way the expectations are set appropriately.

3. Highlight the cost for each of the menu items and portion sizes/combos/customization options.

    For each menu item, have a high-quality food photograph updated on the aggregator platforms. Most of the platforms provide the guidelines on quality and type of food photograph accepted on their platforms. Follow the same but ensure to have attractive food photos for your outlet. Eventually what looks best and delicious in pictures gets sold most.

2. Outlet opening and closing timing:

Once the outlet is listed on the aggregator, the basic information to be provided is outlet's Opening and closing timings. Configure these On and Off time per day of the week accurately and ensure the outlet is marked On and Off at the same time of the day in the aggregator partner application provided to you. This ensures the outlet is shown to the customer as 'available for delivery' when marked On and 'Not available for delivery' when marked OFF. That way you indicate when your outlet is ready or not ready to receive the customers orders. This ensures less chances of order cancellations/rejections if your outlet is not ready but receives the orders and you are unable to process the same.

In case you have a planned weekly off day for the outlet, beforehand configure the Off days in the partner applications. Any holidays for special occasions/festivals need to be marked as OFF days for the outlet (if you plan so) beforehand so that this information is absorbed by the aggregator platforms and accordingly your outlet's availability or non-availability is reflected to the customers.

3. Kitchen Performance Time (KPT): Keep it as low as possible (10-15 mins). Most of the aggregator platforms allow you to configure idle/default kitchen

performance time (KPT) which consists of food preparation time plus order packaging time. Try to keep this time as low as possible, 10-15mins to start with (post that try to reduce the KPT to less than 5 mins).

The outlets with lowest KPT results into minimum delivery time and are preferred by the customers who are looking for the faster delivering outlets.

4. **Mark food ready on time:** As you have set time for food preparation in the aggregator app provided for partners, always ensure to Mark Food Ready for each order to indicate that food was prepared and packed within the time and is ready for handover to delivery partner as soon as he arrives. Marking food ready, indicates to the allocated delivery partner that he should reach to the outlet at the earliest and pick-up the food for delivery.

5. **On time delivery:** Delivery time is the crucial parameter customers look for while placing food orders online. The food delivery time is Food preparation Time by outlet+ delivery time taken by delivery partner between your outlet and customer's delivery location. Now we cannot control the second part of the calculation, but we can minimise the food preparation time at our end. This way the delivery time to end customer can be improvised. Customers would be happy to order food from outlets who deliver faster.

It is very important to deliver the food on-time. The delivery partners on the aggregator platforms get auto-assigned and reach the outlet as per the food preparation time set by your outlet. Please ensure the food, as per the order, has been prepared and packed within the configured food preparation time. Once you mark the order as ready in the aggregator application, the food parcel need to be handed over to the delivery partner within max 3 mins time. Preparing and packing food within stipulated time, marking food ready on time, handing over the food parcel to delivery partner on time so that he can mark the order picked-up from your outlet and travel to the customer's place within the stipulated delivery time based on distance. All these activities are dependant on each other and delay in completion of one activity causes delay in another activity and eventually causing delay in the food delivery to end customer.

If the delivery partner has to wait longer at the outlet to receive the food parcel, leading to delay in food delivery to customer, results into lower customer satisfaction. The food may reach cold/less hot. Your outlet's rating goes down due to delay in handover and marking food ready in the aggregator app. The aggregators also rate the outlet based on these parameters. Eventually, customers rate the outlet based on their overall experience with the outlet which includes food taste and delivery experience. On time delivery ensures high customer satisfaction and high chances of re-orders.

6. Get Max Safety Tag:

Especially during the pandemic time where hygiene and safety was the topmost priority for everyone, the food aggregator platforms also provided the outlets the way to indicate that at your outlet Maximum safety majors are taken care of. To indicate this, the Max Safety Tag was introduced. Get this Tag associated with your outlet by following important health safety and hygiene activities like:

1. Noting down the temperature of staff and updating the same regularly in the partner app of the aggregators.
2. Noting down the temperature of delivery boy whom the food is handed over to and updating the same in the partner app of the aggregators.

7. Ensure the outlet rating on the aggregator platform is maintained at 4+ rating:
Most of the customers before placing the order on an outlet, do check out for the outlet ratings and reviews given by other customers. Hence it is very important to maintain good reviews and ratings on these aggregator platforms. Most of the customers look for 4.0+ rating while shortlisting the outlets to place orders from.

The aggregator platforms calculate the ratings and reviews based on a random algorithm taking into consideration outlet's overall KPT, Food Handover Time, Delivery Time and rating given by the customers.

Customer rating is dependent on the overall food experience and delivery experience via the aggregator platform. The quality and quantity of food served, taste of the food, packaging, portion size are taken into consideration while customer reviews your outlet on these aggregator platforms. With every order dispatched, always ensure to send a hand-written or printed 'Thank You' note to your customers thanking them for the order and request them to rate your outlet and add the reviews on the aggregator platform to encourage you to serve them better.

'Quality and quantity of food was good'.
'The taste was very authentic. Food was fresh and hot'.
'Packaging was superb'
'Portion size was good. Value for money.'
'The thank you note sent along with the parcel was special. Team is innovative and doing great job at building good customer relationship.'

These are some of the review comments we received on aggregator platforms for our outlets. Gives such goosebumps every time we receive a 5* rating and reviews for the service provided.

The overall rating that goes to your outlet is as per algorithm used at respective aggregator's platform. Ensure the outlet's rating is maintained at minimum 4.0* plus out of 5* on each platform where the outlet has been listed. This ensures to build the trust with customers. Customers anticipate the consistency in the service looking at the ratings on these platforms.

8. Run the Ads on food aggregators platforms:

Most of the aggregator platforms provide options to run the commercial advertisement on their platforms. These platforms hold the customer data such as mobile number of the customers so it is easier for them to make your outlet reachable to more customers via the commercial advertisement (paid ads). Once your outlet maintains the ratings of 4.0* plus out of 5*, to reach to more and more customers in your serviceable area from the food aggregator platforms, it is strategically very important step to run the commercial ads on these platforms to reach to more and more customers. Aggregator platforms provide options like CPC (Cost per click) ads, Banner ads, Video Ads. Most used ads are CPC ads. Consult with your outlet's account manager on the respective platform to know more about how to run these ads. Regularly have a check on the performance of these ads to ensure proper ROI (return on investment).

As you continue to follow the above strategies and build a consistent ratings and reviews on the food aggregator platforms, the organic inflow of orders increases automatically as more and more customers know about your food brand.

9. Run promotional offers on food aggregator platform:

Apart from the paid Ads (as explained in point no 8 above), the aggregator platforms also provide ways to create promotional offers like Flat Rs140/- off or 60% Off up to Rs120/- or Free Dish on orders above Rs299/-. Explore the food aggregator partner app to find out the promotional offers provided. Customers are always happy when they get some offer on the orders. They look for the outlets providing offers on these platforms. Do a little bit of research to figure out which offers are being run by the competitor outlets and near by outlets. Choose the best offer applicable for your outlet considering your menu items price range. You would probably have to do menu items pricing accordingly to incur the discount cost. Running promotional offers helps to attract new customers and retain them once they like your food. Even if you discontinue running any paid Ads periodically, the promotional offers along with good ratings helps in attracting more customers organically.

CHAPTER 16

SECRET 16:
HOW TO GROW YOUR CLOUD KITCHEN BUSINESS WITHOUT FOOD AGGREGATORS?

What if the food aggregators platforms are down? Their staff goes on strike and they are not able to deliver the service. Your outlet is out of delivery on these platforms and hence customers are not able to place orders. So, what happens to your food business? Closes completely? I heard you saying, yeah! Not a good sign. Never let your food business be dependent on the aggregator platforms. Your food business should be up and running irrespective of whether aggregators are in operation or not. How is that possible. Want to know the secrets? Let me unfold these pearls of wisdom in this chapter. Stay very focused, this is very important and game changing chapter.

Food business is not just about food. Food business is more of a data business. The one who has more data of target customers, becomes the king of this business. The food aggregator platforms work on this basic. When people download and register on these food aggregator platforms like Zomato and Swiggy, they collect the customer data like Mobile Number and location and push various offers and reminders to get them order food from their platforms. In order to grow big in food business, you need to become king of customer data using which you can offer again and again to the customers about your food, your brand and get them order directly from you.

In this digital era, people are addicted to the social media platforms like FaceBook, Instagram, YouTube and Google. So, the best place to be seen in the eyes of your target customers is the recurring presence of your brand on these social media platforms and attracting the prospective customers using the lucrative offers.

Let us see the secrets of actions required to do so:

1. **Design a Simple and Crazy offer:** Once you have finalized your food niche and the menu items, come up with a simple, lucrative, no brainer offers on a specific food item which is as Crazy as no-brainer offer, so tempting and convincing to the customers that they are bound to give a try to taste your food item at such a crazy offer price. Examples of such crazy offer is Buy1Get1 Free, Get 50% OFF, Buy specific menu item (like Veg Biryani) at Flat Rs99/-

   The crazy offers we designed for our brands:

   Book My Chicken states, Get any chicken dish @ Rs 132/- only , Get Flat 40% discount on your first order.

Make My Fish brand stated, 'Get Two medium slices of Surmai Rawa Fry @ Rs 199/- Only' In the offer, make it very clear to the customer what they would be getting in how much price.

Crazy offer for The Wok Delight 'Get Simply Veg Fried/Steamed Momos (8 pcs) @ 55/- only' Isn't it a no-brainer? The Momos lovers just could not stop visiting our outlet to avail this offer.

Avoid designing offers which are complex to understand for example on orders above Rs 1000/- get free Gulabjamun on two veg Thali. Here it becomes very difficult for the customers to interpret and understand what's being offered. Customer ignores such offers.

Crazy offer we came across was like 'Get Veg Biryani (1 plate) at Rs 39/- 'only. Don't you think, it is so no-brainer offer that anyone would buy it without even trying to know who are you and what brand is it? Here the game was not to make the profit out of the sales (it will be obviously more of a loss) but to get the data of maximum people who will definitely buy your product at such a low price and then reuse the data to pull them to buy again and again from your brand. Obviously, for the customers to keep coming back to you, the food quality, taste, and quantity has to be supreme, for which the customers are sure to order again.

Once you finalize on the crazy offer, have a social media post designed with this offer which should be easy to interpret and with a clear call to action (CTA) for the customers to order and avail the offer. This CTA must be as simple as to call or WhatsApp on your business mobile number. This way customers will be able to reach out to you easily and you will be able to generate leads which you can follow up further to get direct orders.

2. **Create Inaugural offer Google form:** In earlier chapters, we had learnt to use Google Forms to create Survey Form. On Similar basis create the Inaugural offer Google form requesting the prospective customers to fill up the form to avail the offer. This inaugural offer can be the same crazy offer as we discussed in point no1. The offer must be a no-brainer and lucrative for any person that without knowing your brand, people should fill up the form to get the offer. Along with the offer, ask few (max 2 or 3) survey questions like which one is your all-time favourite dish (list few items from your menu), which is your preferred way of ordering food? (Via Zomato, via swiggy, or directly from outlet). Have the mandatory fields like Name, Mobile Number, Email, and Address for you to be able to contact them. The data that you are collecting in this form will help you understand the food eating pattern of the people and will help you to design the next offer posts.

3. **Create Video (short video of max 15 seconds) of crazy offer/inaugural offer:** In today's digital

era, people are more connected and addicted to videos. Create a short video with the food items on which the crazy offer has been based out. The video can cover the short clip of food preparation and tempting final dish that you are offering. You can also showcase yourself talking about your brand and the inaugural offer on launch of your brand. This way your target customer will connect more with you and your brand. Be the face value of your brand.

Now that you have the content ready to collect the customer data and get your initial customers, let us see where should these offers be posted to create the hype of your brand and get the direct orders to your outlet.

1. **WhatsApp groups:** Circulate the Crazy offer post, Inaugural offer Survey form, Inaugural offer Video on WhatsApp with your friends and family members and ask them to circulate it to wider WhatsApp groups in their contacts. Prior to the launch of your brand (at least 15 days before) start creating the hype in your target customers by sharing these people puller offers, not all together at once, but with a gap of few days. Circulate the offer posts, videos and inaugural offer survey form on your society WhatsApp groups and request them to share and circulate it to wider WhatsApp groups in their contacts. WhatsApp is most used tool for connecting with people directly.

Your brand's hype creation starts even before launch and you will have few direct customers on the launch day to avail the crazy/inaugural offer. Isn't it crazy? Using the same method, we got minimum 45 orders on the launch day of our brands and that was a confidence booster sale. Thank you, God!

2. **FaceBook groups:** Circulate the crazy offer post, Inaugural offer Survey Form and Video on FaceBook groups where your target audience is found. Now people don't know about you and your brand, but they will still fill up the survey form and contact you for orders due to the crazy, no-brainer offer. This also helps in creating hype, showing creativity of your brand even before the launch of the brand. Go aggressive on hype creation and you will get the data as people fill up the survey form or contact you directly via call/WhatsApp. Surely, the orders are ensured on the launch day! Hurry!

3. **YouTube Channel:** We learnt in earlier chapter, to create YouTube channel of your brands. Having created that, post the Inaugural offer video on the YouTube channel in the form of Shorts or Video. Use the appropriate Hashtags to make it viral. Circulate the links of the YouTube shorts and videos on Facebook groups, WhatsApp groups and make them viral. Enquiry calls, WhatsApp messages and orders are sure to come on the launch day or even prior to that.

4. **Instagram profile of Brand:** We created the Instagram profile of the brand. Post the crazy offer post, Inaugural offer video as Instagram Reel and Instagram Story. Use the appropriate Hashtags to make it viral. In the Instagram profile, in the description section, have the crazy offer highlighted and CTA (call to action) stating call/WhatsApp <your business mobile number> to avail the offer. Isn't it easy?? Enjoy the direct orders flowing in.

5. **Facebook page of Brand:** In earlier chapters, we spoke about creating Facebook page of your brand. Post the crazy offer post, Inaugural offer video and the Google form with Inaugural offer survey periodically on this Facebook Page. Also post it in Facebook Story, Facebook Reel. Use the appropriate Hashtags to make it viral. Circulate these posts periodically on different Facebook groups where your target audience is found. This helps in hype creation of your brand and people visit to your Facebook page more often increasing the engagement with your brand.

6. **Google My Business (GMB):** In earlier chapters, we learnt about creating Google My Business profile for your brand. On this GMB page, post the Crazy Offer post, upload the menu card images and video of Inaugural offer. It helps for hype creation and your target audience connects with you on call/WhatsApp to get the offers.

7. **Run paid Facebook and Instagram Ads:** Using the crazy offer post and Inaugural offer video, create the paid advertisement which runs on both Facebook and Instagram. Be specific about selecting your target audience age group, area of residence within 4 km of your outlet and identifying the target audience based on their specific interests (such as specific food niche items like momos, pizza, chicken food and so on.) There are many articles on how to run Facebook and Instagram Ads. Refer to those articles by doing a Google search. These are paid Ads and Facebook charges for the Ads based on your per day budget to run the Ad. In the given budget you can configure to run the same Ad on Facebook as well as Instagram.

    Run two different Ads for crazy offer post and Inaugural offer video as the media type is different. Facebook paid Ads are effective tools via which interested target audience connects with the business via Call or WhatsApp or you can take them to your ordering website (or food aggregator's ordering link) or on the lead generation form (similar to the Google survey form).

    These are various ways to collect the data of customers and get the direct orders. With Facebook and Instagram Ads, you get instant orders or you get instant data to follow up and convert the leads into orders. Based on the ROI (return on investment) of the paid Ads, and based on your budget, you can decide how long you want to run these ads. The paid ads are the best way to generate the leads of interested customers in your food brand and convert these leads into actual orders by constantly nurturing them over a period. Patience is the key!

8. **Run paid Google Ads:** Like Facebook and Instagram Ads, Google also gives an option for creating Google Ads based on keywords. Most of the people use Google to find out best place to get specific food around them. Using the most searched keywords as analysed by Google, create the Google Ads to stay on Top of the search and highlight your brand more prominently whenever your target audience is searching for food in your area of service. There are many tutorials available on Google to know how to configure the Google Ads. Depending on your budget and ROI (return on Investment) decide on how long to run these ads. Patience is the key!

9. **Use the Instagram Influencers, food bloggers to promote the Inaugural offer:** In this digital era, where people are addicted to the social media platforms, many Instagram influencers and food bloggers have their fan followings on Instagram and Facebook. Look for the Instagram Influencers and/or food bloggers with forty thousand plus followers. Invite the Instagram influencers and food bloggers to your outlet and share your prime food dishes. They make

short videos of these food items, make reels which can be promoted on their Instagram and Facebook page tagging your brand's Instagram profile. Have your crazy offer circulated or posted on their Instagram Story for wider reach.

10. **Convert the Aggregator customers into direct ordering customers:** In earlier chapters, we have seen how to grow the business on food aggregators. As you start getting orders from Food aggregator platforms, use this opportunity to convert these customers into your direct ordering customers. People who are ordering online using food aggregator platforms are NOT your customers, they are customers of these aggregator platforms. The aggregator platforms are great source of getting leads of the target customers. The aggregator platforms will take away their commission charges from your profit margins. Instead, take efforts to convert these customers into your direct orders by using any of the following methods:

A. **Send the crazy offer pamphlets** or your menu card pamphlet along with the food parcel. Looking at your crazy offer which is so lucrative, that next time the customer will call or WhatsApp you directly to place the orders.

B. **Send a Thank You note** along with the food parcel and request the customer to rate your service on food aggregator platforms and share the screenshot on your WhatsApp number. On doing this, give a lucrative offer to the customer on his next direct order with you. This way, you get good ratings and reviews for your brand on the aggregator platforms and as the customer WhatsApp you the screenshot, you get their direct number to connect on and give the offer. Later, you can keep pushing the offer posts and keep getting the direct orders.

C. **Call a customer:** Most of the aggregator platforms provide an option to call the customer whose order is in progress (Zomato, MagicPin provide this option, Swiggy does not!) Make a call to customer using the aggregator platform, and give them an update about their order, such as 'order is ready to dispatch or has been dispatched via delivery partner' and pitch in the conversation to let them know that you also provide the delivery service and they can order directly from the outlet. Ask for their WhatsApp number to share your menu card. 99% of the customers will share their WhatsApp number during this conversation. Use this data to connect with the customer directly, share your menu card and crazy offer details on WhatsApp. 80% of the customers order directly when they want to order next from you. To gain the trust of the customer always maintain the food quality and taste to high level and ensure smooth delivery experience. Consistency plays a major role.

Secrets behind making Customers for Life (CFL):

Once the customer orders food from your outlet, take efforts to make them your customers for life. Here are some effective ways to do so:

1. Always give 10X value compare to the money the customer is paying for the food.

2. Always respect making small money, because small money becomes big money. We had a customer who visited our outlet to purchase a low value food item. We respected his purchase. Later, this customer went on purchasing food amounting to value of Rs1000/- per month. That is called making customers for Life. So always respect making small money.

3. Always maintain the food quality and taste above standards.

   Do not compromise on the quality and quantity of food. Some outlets reduce the quantity of food when giving crazy offers. Avoid doing that.

4. Although with crazy offer, the profit margins are less, focus on getting the lead and initial direct orders which are confidence boosters. Using the lead information, you can always pull the customers later with various other

offers. With consistent better service, the customers become loyal customers of your brand for Life.

5. Constantly keep the customers/direct leads engaged with your brand by once in a week offer post circulated on WhatsApp, involving them in activities like quizzes and giving away awards (free dish, free delivery and so on).

6. Encourage customers to take photos of your food dishes along with your brand logo and post it on their social media profiles like Facebook and Instagram and tag your brand's profile. On doing this, offer them free dish or free delivery based on your budget and profit margins. This way, the customers are engaged with your brand and your brand's innovative ideas. Brand building and marketing happens as they post the food photos with your brand logo and/or their selfie with your food.

7. Encourage customers to put their reviews online using the Google My Business review link and on your own website for ordering, if any. This helps to build customer trust when the other target audience look for reviews about your brand or food niche and come across good reviews. On doing this, offer them free delivery or free dish, based on your budget, on their next order. This works wonderfully.

8. Make the offer posts for the combo offers, bulk or party packages, festival offers and circulate to the contacts/

leads, Facebook Groups and WhatsApp groups. This helps to get recurring business from existing customers. Party orders, bulk orders are the major source of big profits. Focus on getting more party/bulk orders for profitable business.

CHAPTER 17

SECRET 17: EFFECTIVE STRATEGIES OF MARKETING TO GROW THE SALES

'We saw your advertisement on Instagram and came looking for your outlet.' 'We see your regular food posts on Facebook and Instagram, they are quite impressive. The food looks delicious. I had a wish to visit your outlet, and today I am fulfilling the same.' 'I searched for best seafood nearby my area, and your outlet Make My Fish was listed on top. I directly rushed to your outlet after checking your reviews.'

These are the actual quotes from our customers who visited our outlet and expressed how did they find out our outlet. Such an overwhelming experience and proud moment! I heard you saying 'wow.' The strategies we had used to get this attention from the target market has been revealed in this chapter. Let us get into the secrets. Stay focused.

17.1. Digital (Online) marketing

In this vast evolving digital era, online (digital) marketing is must. Let us see 8 ways of Digital Marketing that will help reach to wider audience and boost your sales.

1. **WhatsApp Business:** The commonly used tool for the direct and quick communication, in today's digital era is WhatsApp. WhatsApp has two versions; one is regular and another is WhatsApp Business. Upgrade the WhatsApp on your business mobile number to WhatsApp Business version to use its powerful tools.

   In the about section, add short description and crazy offer in short. Update the business timings, update an order taking website, if any or use your business Facebook or Instagram profile link, update the catalogue with the menu items images and details. Update your brands logo or attractive food image as your WhatsApp profile picture.

   Keep your direct leads who connects with you on WhatsApp engaged with your brand by consistently updating the WhatsApp status with engaging contents like lucrative offer posts, food images, phots of packaged food ready to parcel, short video of recipe making along with a trendy music/song, customer testimonials, reviews. Customers connect with you and your brand instantly and remember of you when they want to order food. Also, they recommend your brand to their friends and families as they keep seeing your consistent efforts and growth of your brands.

2. **Google My Business:** More and more people use Google search to figure out on best place to get a specific cuisine (food niche) in their locality. It is must to have your business listed on Google My Business to get listed in search results. Customers may not know your brand name, but they know what they want to eat. Customers look for specific cuisine/dish name in the search criteria like 'best Chinese near me', 'best seafood in Thane', 'Best place to get chicken dishes near me'. While describing your business, use the keywords that the customers are likely to use in their searches. Also update the menu, food photos, address, location details, contact number and timings of your business for people to reach out to your outlet easily. Only creating the Google My Business listing is not enough, it needs to be kept active by regular updates of offer posts, customer feedback videos, short videos of your food recipes, short video clips of your kitchen insights or surroundings. Encourage your customers to leave Google Review on your GMB profile. All this will help to stay on top of the search results when customers are looking for best cuisines (food niche) in the nearby locality. If your brand gets listed in top 5 of the search results and has great reviews, then there are high chances to get the business from that customer.

So many times, we heard from our direct customers that we searched for best seafood near me and your brand 'Make My Fish' came on top. That is how we called up your outlet and are ordering from you.

So many times, we heard from our customers that we searched for best chicken dishes in thane and your brand 'Book My Chicken' was listed in top. And your reviews are great. So, we called up your outlet and are ordering from you. Hope you provide home delivery?'

Words are not enough to describe how proud feeling we get when we are showered with this love and appreciation. All the efforts put in to create the Google My Business profile are worth it as we keep getting customers and business from there.

Google does not charge anything for the listing of business on GMB.

3. **Instagram Profile:** For each of your brand, it is must to have a profile on Instagram. Instagram is one of the favourite App/Tool used in this digital era. Create an attractive Instagram Profile and upgrade it to business profile (from settings option). Use your brand's logo in the Instagram profile display image. Give a short and effective description of your brand highlighting the speciality, crazy offer for customers, contact details, order taking website (if not your own website, you can give food aggregator ordering link) for the customers to place direct orders.

Instagram profile need to be regularly updated with food photos, offer posts, short videos of your food recipes/preparations, short videos of your customers unboxing your food parcel, short videos of your customers eating your food and giving feedback, most trending memes around your food niche and so on.

Let me tell you real incident. When a customer visited our outlet, he showed us the seafood photos from our Instagram profile of our brand 'Make My Fish' and said *'I had saved these photos in my Instagram profile as my wish list of outlets to visit. I am completing my wish list by visiting Make My Fish today.'* Wow! Feeling. Truly humbled and grateful to our loyal and esteemed customers.

Instagram reels are most popular means of reaching to wider audiences. These days videos are more attention seekers than the normal photos or posts. Be consistent in creating the short videos of the food recipes, customer feedback, unboxing of food parcel and use the trending music on Instagram to create the attractive reels. There are many free video editing tools such as InShot, available which can be used to edit these videos quickly and upload on brand's Instagram profile with proper hashtags. Instagram reels has wider reach and goes viral quickly. This is a powerful tool to connect with your target audience without paying any cost. This is called Free Marketing.

A customer visiting our outlet showed us our reel on Chicken Biryani from Instagram profile of 'Book My Chicken' and placed order for 2Kg chicken biryani for a family gathering. Efforts in making the reel were worth! Without spending money, getting customers via free online marketing.

4. **Instagram Food Influencer:** Instagram Influencers are the personalities with great fan following on Instagram. They are popular and their fans look up to their recommendations to try out things they promote. Look out for the Instagram food influencers with minimum forty thousand plus (for metro cities) fan following from your local area on Instagram. Reach out to these food influencers for a collaboration to promote your brand. Most of the food influencers work on barter collaboration, where in exchange of free food, they promote your brand and food on their Instagram profile and stories. Some of the food influencers charge a certain amount from you to promote your brand's food photos or short videos as reels on their Instagram profile, stories. These influencers visit your outlet to take short videos while the food items are being prepared and served.

This activity helps in reaching out to their wider audiences quickly and helps in increased enquiries and orders or customer visits to your outlet.

5. **Facebook and Instagram Ad:** Most of your target audience is on Facebook and Instagram these days. Make use of these great platforms to connect directly with your target customers. Facebook Ad Manager is a business tool provided by Facebook which allows to run paid advertisement on both Facebook and Instagram platforms. Create the attractive offer posts, crazy offer videos and use these media to create and configure the Facebook and Instagram advertisements. Configure the ads to target your specific customer, in your target areas of service (within 4km from your outlet location), identify the target audience basis their age group, common interests related to the food niche. Ad configured on Facebook can also run on Instagram platform. These paid ads are very powerful tool to get direct orders, direct leads and to stay in front of your target audiences online. The direct leads acquired using these ads need to nurtured to convert into orders. Patience is the key. Since these are paid marketing avenues, keep a check on ROI (Return on Investment) and see which offer is grabbing more attention, audience reach and orders. Basis the ROI, decide on doubling up or going down on this marketing avenue.

6. **Aggregator Ad:** Most of the people use food aggregator platforms like Zomato and Swiggy to order food online. When people want to order food, the definite place they check out for food are these food aggregator platforms. These platforms give various

options to run the commercial advertisement like Pay Per Click (PPC) ads, Banner Ads, Video Ads. Make use of these advertisements on these popular aggregator platforms to use their customer database and reach to more and more target audiences. More orders you get, higher the chances to get their data for your usage. Use this data (their mobile number) to nurture them with your food offers and eventually convert them into your direct customers. We discussed more on how to convert the aggregator customers into your direct customers in the earlier chapter as well. Again, keep a check on the ROI (return on investment) on running these paid ads on aggregator platforms to double up or go down on this investment. Look at this investment to gain more of customer data along side the orders. Although the profit margin is less in case of aggregator orders, as these platforms take away their commissions from your profit, still they are powerful tool to generate direct leads along with the revenue.

7. **Repeat Orders:** It is far easier to sell to your existing customers than acquiring a new customer to buy your products. So nurture your current customers who have bought your food items at least once and the direct leads (who have shown interest in your brand but have not yet purchased anything) by sending lucrative offer posts regularly on WhatsApp (not daily, otherwise chances are high that they will block your business number from their contact list.). Once in a week is fine. Send festival

greetings occasionally. Send the bulk or party order posts to grab big orders. This is very effective way of getting repeat business from your existing database of leads.

8. **Google Ads:** Paid advertisement on Google is very effective way of digital marketing. Considering the fact that your target audience is definitely going to reach out to Google to look for the best food options in their nearby locality. Use this opportunity to present your brand on top in their search results. This is achieved by using the Google Ads. Use most frequently used keywords as recommended by Google to configure the Google Ads, specify the target audience age groups, interests, and area (within 4km area from your outlet), use a crazy offer media (post or video) to get the attention and the order from target customer. Keep a check on the ROI (return on investment) and decide when to double up or go down on the investment. For the Google Ad marketing to be more effective, ensure your Google My Business profile is updated with latest contact number, address and location of your business for your customers to reach out your business quickly. Ensure GMB is updated with latest menu, food images, offer posts and has Google Ratings at least 4plus.

17.2. Traditional (Offline) Marketing

Although digital era is booming, the traditional/offline marketing also plays a major role to get you the business.

Still a lot of population is used to the traditional ways. Let us refer to four interesting ways of traditional marketing to grab the attention of your target market and eventually grow your sales.

1. **Pamphlets:** Distributing pamphlets of your brand's menu cards, offer posts in the nearby areas of your outlet where your target audience is found is one of the most popular and effective traditional/offline marketing strategy. Along with the menu card, highlight the crazy offer to grab the attention of your target customers. Basis the crazy offer, the audience will connect with you either for an enquiry or for an order.

   Put in efforts to figure out which area, societies, offices to cover so that maximum of your target audience is covered. Your personal involvement is required to ensure the printed copies are distributed at the destined places through proper channels. Use the local news paper agencies distribution links, use the people who specifically do pamphlet distribution work. Depending on the ROI (Return on Investment), double up or go down on this marketing channel.

2. **Standees, Flyers, and boards:** Around the places where your target audience is found such as schools, colleges, Gyms, Public Garden area, Societies, Society club houses, commercial complexes, offices, figure out a way to put up the standees or flyers or boards of your

food brand along with lucrative crazy offer and contact details to order. These are also effective ways to do brand marketing and get the direct orders.

3. **Word of Mouth/ Referrals:** Launch a referral scheme for your current customers stating if they refer your brand to their families and friends and if the order is placed via their reference, the referee and referral both will get a certain percentage of discount. This way mouth publicity of your brand is spread a fast and helps in getting direct orders.

4. **Posters on Cabs, Taxies, Buses:** In most of the Tier1 and Tier2 cities, the latest trend of offline marketing is to use the local cabs, autos, taxies, or public transport buses to host your brands hording/posters. Ensure to have brand logo, name, clear and simple offer, contact details of your business on the poster for customers to reach out to your business. Enquire for the agencies in your area/city who does this work for you. JustDial.com will help to get you these contacts. Depending on your marketing budget, decide on the numbers and approach. This is one of the most effective ways to get noticed prominently in public domain. This helps greatly in brand building and marketing of your brands.

Huh! Bulb On! So many avenues to reach out to your target audience. Marketing is like breathing. Your business is alive, if you are continuously investing in marketing. Having underlystood these pearls of wisdom of marketing, list down which of the marketing avenues are you going to use prominently. Put the marketing budget in place and get the rewards of return on investments. Congratulations for the super-duper sales.

What are the secrets of making big money? How does the brand become scalable and profitable? Getting these questions? You should. Of course, we know the secrets behind making it BIG! Meet me in next chapter where I unfold secrets of ultimate food business funnel for a profitable cloud kitchen business. See you there.

CHAPTER 18

SECRET 18: ULTIMATE FOOD BUSINESS FUNNEL FOR A PROFITABLE CLOUD KITCHEN BUSINESS

'We have shifted our residence to another area in Mumbai, your food is good, do you have plans to open a branch in this area?. You should.' 'I am big fan of your food, consistently providing quality and tasty food. If you ever think of franchising your brand, do consider me first in the line to grab your brand's franchises'

These are the actual quotes from loyal customers of our brands. What a great moment! What a proud feeling of starting something which is worth enough. We are really humbled. Let us see the secrets of building this trust, repo, and image about your brands into the market.

For the passion for food and getting into entrepreneurship, we started off with the cloud kitchen business wherein we sale a specific cuisine food and give service in exchange of money. We cannot grow big just by selling per day food items. Food business is not about just food, its about data. The one who has more data, he/she becomes King/Queen of the business. More data means more customers/leads. More the customers and leads, again and again you can nurture them in long run and get repeat orders, bulk orders. From these repeat customers only, people who see the consistency and values in your brands and who are interested for getting into food business, will come forward to take franchise of your brands. This is where we start making big money. We can not make profits just by selling food from per day orders, we need to sale brand to make it big. To be successful in this business, focus more on brand building. **Ultimately selling your brand's franchises, multiple outlets in multiple locations will fetch you more profit.**

1. Go Multi brand:

We learnt in the earlier chapters to have specific food niche-based brand. With this micro niche based brand, you target a specific target market. By targeting again and again to this market, you get a recurring business. However, to grow big, we also need to cover other target markets who are looking for other types of food. That is where multi-branding comes into picture. If you are a new entrant in food business, always start with a single brand, targeting a specific target market. Once you make a sale of minimum up to Rs 2.5 Lacs in 3 to 6 months' time (depending on your marketing budget), you must consider launching your next brand which is again based on a micro-niche, targeting another market segment. Now the food segment for your next brand can be or need not be completely new but can be derived from your current brand's food category.

For Example, you have a brand with micro niche as Biryani. There are different target markets to sell the Biryani to. To target the premium customers, have a premium Biryani brand with a premium brand name, premium logo, premium packaging, more quantity, higher cost. To target a lower/middle class customer, have another brand which will have brand name which connects with the mass, has lower value packaging, less quantity with appropriate costing.

So, with the same kitchen setup, using same staff, same food inventory, you can target entire market with all segments of customers covered. You need to have different strategy for marketing to target that specific customer audience with that specific Biryani Brand.

The company called Rebel foods is successfully running two brands of Biryani as 'Behrouz Biryani,' targeting the premium segment and 'The Biryani Life,' targeting the lower/middle class segment of the market.

The same logic can be applied to other food niches. If you have a Chinese brand running successfully targeting Chinese cuisine lovers and in your existing brand, you have varieties of Momos getting sold as best sellers then why not have a Momos special brand? With Momos special brand, you will be able to attract Momos lovers with appropriate marketing. With two brands, now you have Chinese lovers customer base and Momos lovers customer base. It is far easy to cross sale your products to these to different customer bases.

Suppose you start with third brand which is completely into a different cuisine, say varieties of Thali, then your already built two customer bases will be your ready audience to sell the Thalis too. Of course, a Chinese lover would have requirement for Thali, a momos lover would have requirement for Thali for his family. This cross selling is more effective as your existing customers already know the quality of food and service provided by your brands. It is much easier to sell them your next product from your next brand than acquiring a completely new customer to your brands.

When we started with our first brand, Book My Chicken, which has chicken specials as micro-niche, the customers of Book My Chicken started demanding for Seafood verities as well. That is how we tabbed on this demand and designed our next brand, Make My Fish, with micro-niche as Seafood. The very first customers for Make My Fish were from the customer database of Book My Chicken. Of course, we have separate marketing budget for Make My Fish to target the seafood lover's audience. This way we got growing chicken lover's customer database with incremental marketing strategies and we also got growing seafood lover's customer database with separate marketing strategy. It was much easier to cross-sale the chicken special and seafood specials to these two growing databases.

With Book My Chicken and Make My Fish, the family audience was getting covered. To target the younger crowd (age group from 18yrs to 35 years) we tapped on the market survey and covered the Chinese food niche to target this audience. That is how we started with our third brand The Wok Delight. Along with new customer database that we attracted using marketing strategy for The Wok Delight, the existing customers from Book My Chicken and Make My Fish were delighted to have more food varieties in terms of the Chinese food. That helped to increase the order value for their chicken special and seafood special orders by adding one or more Chinese food variety for some of their family members. This is how it helps to grow and get more business with multi-brands.

The point here is to go multi brand. Each brand needs to be micro-niche oriented and for each brand have a specific marketing budget and strategy. To summarize, the benefits of having multiple brands in a cloud kitchen are:

1. **Increased revenue potential:** By offering multiple brands with specific micro-niche, targeting specific market, a cloud kitchen can attract a wider range of customers and thus increases its revenue potential.

2. **Efficient use of kitchen resources:** In a cloud kitchen setup, it is easier to use its resources more efficiently by preparing and delivering multiple brands from a single kitchen setup unless you need a completely different cookware to prepare your specific food niche.

3. **Reduced costs:** By sharing resources (cookware and kitchen staff) and space, a cloud kitchen greatly reduces its costs and increases its profitability.

4. **Manifolded revenue streams:** Multiple brands provide a diversified revenue stream and reduce the risk of depending on a single brand's success.

5. **Increased brand exposure and cross selling:** Offering multiple brands increase a cloud kitchen's brand exposure, leading to more customers and greater opportunities for cross-selling of the brand's food items to different customer bases leading to higher revenues.

6. **Flexibility and Adaptability:** Multi-brand cloud kitchens quickly adapt to changing market trends and customers preferences by adding or removing the brands as necessary.

All your food brands come under one umbrella of your parent Food Company. Like, our brands Book My Chicken, Make My Fish, and The Wok Delight come under Sabrosoo Foods Company. With multi brands, the valuation of the company Sabrosoo Foods manifolds. Provided the quality of food, taste of the menu items and quality of service given to the customers is consistent.

2: Multiple sources of income per brand

For each of the brand, in multi-brand scenarios, following check-points are must to ensure each brands' revenue potential is manifolded.

1. **Effective niche specific Brand Name:** Strong and niche-oriented brand name (we already covered more on this in earlier chapters.) This reduces your marketing cost greatly.

2. **Menu and Pricing:** Limited (10 to 15 menu items maximum) and pricing according to the target market.

3. **Packaging:** Suitable, attractive, and effective packaging based on target market segment.

4. **Quality:** Consistency in quality and taste of food served.

5. **Delivery:** Effective and quick delivery service in place.

6. **Marketing:** Continuous marketing with constant check on ROI (Return on Investment) to double up or zero down on the marketing budget.

7. **Multiple income model:** For each of the brand, have following channels to sell the food to increase the revenue exponentially.

   1. **Via aggregators:** Orders processed via food aggregator platforms (refer to the earlier chapter on how to grow orders on aggregators).

   2. **Via direct orders:** Orders processed via direct customers (refer to the earlier chapter on how to grow business with direct customers.)

   3. **Via party/bulk orders:** Orders processed for big events like family gatherings, birthday parties, Marriage functions and so on.

4. **Via subscription/ Wallet system:** Offering subscription or wallet system to the direct customers where in the customers pay you in advance for the specified time service (such as for fifteen days, for one month, quarterly and so on.) This way, customers pay you in advance and remain with your brand for longer association. Resulting into the recurring business.

5. **Via B2B orders: Business to Business orders:** Businesses like corporate hubs, government offices, private organizations (IT or Non-IT) where hundreds of people work together are the best sources to get the regular/bulk orders. Tie-up with the such businesses to get regular or party (event based) orders.

6. **Franchise/multiple outlets:** On scaling up the business revenue and establishing your brand over a period, the demand for franchise starts pouring in. Plan for expansion to multiple locations within and/or multiple cities. With multiple outlets and franchises, the revenue potential manifolds to a different level altogether.

Ultimately with a strong preparation to build solid brand/s, right launch plan, Quality products, right strategies to scale up the revenue leading to franchise demands, results into 10X valuation to your food business company. Revenue targets of Rs 10 lacs to Rs 1 crore per month has been achieved using same fundamentals.

Now that you are aware of all 18 secrets on how to Build, Launch and Scale your cloud kitchen to make it profitable within 90 days, note down all the secrets and your brands compatibility against each secret. While doing this exercise, evaluate where you need to score more, where you need to put in more efforts to achieve the results. Surely, you will lead your food business to make it profitable. Have that confidence and patience!

Looking forward to see your brands achieving and embarking more revenue heights. Congratulations in advance.

In my next book, I will focus more on Franchise models and Expansions with multiple outlets in multiple cities resulting into multiplying your revenues to multi-crore business.